Wesker
the Playwright

GLENDA LEEMING

METHUEN . LONDON AND NEW YORK

First published in 1983 in simultaneous hardback and paperback editions in Great Britain by Methuen London Ltd, 11 New Fetter Lane, London EC4P 4EE, and in the United States of America by Methuen Inc, 733 Third Avenue, New York, NY 10017

Copyright © 1983 by Glenda Leeming

ISBN 0 413 49230 3 (Hardback)
ISBN 0 413 49240 0 (Paperback)

Printed and bound in Great Britain by
Butler & Tanner Ltd, Frome and London

Contents

Abbreviations and Sources

ABBREVIATIONS

FF: Arnold Wesker, *Fears of Fragmentation*
JJ: Arnold Wesker, *Journey into Journalism*
LL: Arnold Wesker, *Love Letters on Blue Paper and Other Stories*
P&P: *Plays and Players*
SS: Arnold Wesker, *Six Sundays in January*
TQ: *Theatre Quarterly*
TW: Charles Marowitz and Simon Trussler (eds.), *Theatre at Work*

SOURCES

References in the text to Wesker's plays are to the four-volume Penguin edition (see Bibliography) for instance, III 126 refers to page 126 of Volume 3, and so on. The exception is *Caritas*, where page numbers are those of the Cape edition (1981). Unattributed quotations from Wesker himself are from letters, interviews, diaries and other unpublished material generously made available to the author by Arnold Wesker. Contemporary reviews of productions are attributed to writer or journal in the text, as are certain major interviews and articles; the remainder are attributed in the Notes.

List of Illustrations

Note: all the photographs come from Arnold Wesker's own collection, and I am very grateful to him for his generosity in lending them. Where no credit is given, either the pictures were taken privately or I have not been able to trace the photographer. G.L.

Arnold Wesker—Chronology

1932 Born in East End of London: father, Joseph Wesker, a Russian-Jewish tailor; mother, Leah Wesker, Hungarian-Jewish.

1939 Evacuated briefly to various parts of England and Wales, but spent most of the war period at home. Lived with parents when in London until his marriage.

1943 Failed eleven plus, and went to Upton House Central School, which emphasized clerical studies. Enjoyed amateur acting outside school.

1948 Left school and worked at many jobs, including carpenter's mate, bookseller's assistant and plumber's mate.

1950–52 Two years National Service in the Royal Air Force. Formed drama group for enlisted airmen. Wrote a series of diary-style letters intending to reshape them as a novel, but which were actually used as the raw material for *Chips With Everything*.

1952–56 Several jobs in Norfolk - seed sorter, farm labourer, kitchen porter - then returned to London, where he spent two years as a pastry cook.

1956 Worked in Paris for nine months as a chef, saving money to enter the London School of Film Technique.

1957 Met Lindsay Anderson by chance and asked him to read his short story *Pools*, as possible subject for a film. Although this came to nothing, Anderson read *Chicken Soup With Barley* and *The Kitchen* and sent them to George Devine at the Royal Court Theatre.

1958 First production of *Chicken Soup With Barley* directed by John Dexter at the Belgrade Theatre, Coventry. This transferred to London to the Royal Court for a second week, then to the West End. Awarded Arts Council grant of £300, which he used to marry Doreen Bicker, whom he had met while both were working in a Norfolk hotel.

1959 *Roots* and *The Kitchen* first produced. *Evening Standard*'s Most Promising Playwright Award.

1960 *Chicken Soup With Barley, Roots* and *I'm Talking About Jerusalem* produced as *The Wesker Trilogy* at the Royal Court, opening on 7 June, 28 June, and 27 July respectively.

1961 *Roots* was Wesker's first play to be produced in the USA: the off-Broadway production received mixed notices. *The Kitchen:* revised version staged at Royal Court, and film version released. Demonstrated against use of nuclear weapons along with other writers, and sentenced to one month in prison. Accepted directorship of Centre Fortytwo, a cultural movement for making the arts more widely accessible, primarily through trade union support and involvement.

1962 *Chips With Everything* opened and voted Best Play of 1962. Wesker inaugurated simultaneous productions in the provinces, with openings in Glasgow and Sheffield a few days after the London premiere. *Chips* transferred to West End.

1963 *Chips With Everything* opened on Broadway to good notices. *Menace* on BBC-TV.

1964 *Their Very Own and Golden City* won Italian Premio Marzotto drama award.

1965 Off-Broadway production of *The Kitchen* achieved a six-month run to good notices. *The Four Seasons* opened at the Belgrade, Coventry, transferred to West End.

1966 *Their Very Own and Golden City:* world premiere in Belgium, then British premiere at Royal Court.

1967 Off-Broadway production of *The Four Seasons*: badly received.

1970 After directing his own *The Friends* first in Stockholm then at the Roundhouse, Wesker resigned from the Roundhouse Trust and on 20 December persuaded the Council for Centre Fortytwo to pass a resolution dissolving itself.

1972 *The Old Ones* opened at Royal Court.

1973 *The Kitchen* won gold medal in Spain.

1974 *The Old Ones* well received in a workshop production off-Broadway. *The Wedding Feast:* world premiere in Stockholm.

1976 Sales of the Penguin edition of *The Wesker Trilogy* reached quarter of a million. BBC-1 TV presentation of *Love Letters on Blue Paper*. World premiere of *The Merchant* at the Stockholm Royal Dramaten, 8 October.

1977 British premiere of *The Wedding Feast*, Leeds Playhouse, 20 January. World premiere of *The Journalists* at the Criterion Theatre, Coventry (amateur production), 26 March. World premiere of *Love Letters on Blue Paper*, Syracuse (USA). English-speaking premiere of *The Merchant*, New York, 16 November.

1978 *The Merchant*: British premiere, Birmingham Repertory Theatre, 12 October. *Love Letters on Blue Paper* opened at the National Theatre's Cottesloe auditorium, directed by the author, 15 February.

1979 *Chicken Soup* wins gold medal as best foreign play at National Theatre Madrid. Wesker commissioned to write film script of the *Trilogy*, financed by National Film Development Fund.

1980 Commissioned by the touring theatres of Norway, Sweden and Denmark to write a new play: this play, *Caritas*, completed in July. *One More Ride on the Merry-Go-Round* written under a pseudonym in 1978 now revised and pseudonym dropped. Original film script, *Lady Othello*, written, and TV play, *Whitsun*, adapted from story *The Visit*.

1981 Premiere of *Caritas* at the National Theatre's Cottesloe auditorium on 7 October. Professional premiere of *The Journalists* 10 October at Wilhelmshaven, Germany. First draft of *Breakfast*, short play for television. Adaptation of *The Four Seasons* for television. First draft of one-act comedy, *Sullied Hands*.

1982 *Mothers*, a set of four portraits on the theme of the mother, commissioned by Koichi Kimura for Tokyo festival of one-act plays, where it was premiered 2 July, directed by Tsunetoshi Hirowatarai.

1

A Personal Tone of Voice

I have attempted many times to talk with myself and ask why and how. But I know that I forget ... in fact, one forgets all the books that one reads, and I have got a terrible memory, anyway. So that sometimes I express an opinion and forget the justification for it, and the reason why it's part of me: but it didn't form entirely out of the air, it formed because of so many things that have happened, and books that I have read. But I forget. (TQ 28 pp. 78-9)

Of all modern dramatists Arnold Wesker must be one of the most – if not *the* most – personally involved in his own work, even though, of all literary forms, drama offers least opportunity for this kind of authorial subjectivity.

As Wesker says, 'I don't know what it's like for other writers, but for me the bits and pieces of myself are in different characters'. At one time he believed strongly that the work and life of any artist should be seen as a whole; that knowledge of a writer's life gave the right perspective to his public utterances, whether dramatic or academic. He explained in a lecture in 1968:

I feel a compulsion to tell you more about myself and so I shall punctuate this lecture with a personal tone, so that you understand and judge better what I say, and are reminded that a fallible man is speaking. It is not simply that it is inadequate to stand before you and offer thoughts if you don't know why those thoughts are offered, but also because those of us who dare to speak before people must choose our words with care and honesty, and that is not easy and I want you to know that I know it is not easy. (FF p. 105)

One of his own characters, Mary Mortimer in *The Journalists*, demolishes just such a statement from a public speaker with 'Really! Who does he think he is? Protesting his imperfections as though we wouldn't believe he had any in the first place' (IV 50). Wesker has always attracted this sort of exasperated hostility, so it was not without some personal feeling that he remarked later in the same lecture:

In this life some things must remain sacred or we will destroy our

1

humanity, and one of the things that should remain sacred is the nerve-racking sight of a vulnerable man exposing his confusions wounds or despair, or simply singing hymns of praise at being alive. (FF p. 121)

Yet the reaction of people who actually meet him face to face is that of the lady journalist who arrived pre-programmed to do a hatchet job and departed, won over, crying 'I can't, I can't. He's genuine, talked to me like an equal'. Indeed he protested later that he was 'rather fed up with being told how sweet and lovable I am, because there are many sides to me'. The 'sweet and lovable' label invites patronage, and the personal tone in public speaking and writing provokes embarrassment – and a defensive hostility. And when the personal tone appears in the plays, even as the personal tone of a character, very often the reaction is the same. Wesker suggests 'There is a quality in my writing which makes it very un-English and which comes from my Jewish-European back-ground'.[1] This is probably close to the truth – the quality is a verbal equivalent of body-language by which, it is said, Italians can bear standing closer to each other than Americans, and Americans tolerate greater closeness than the literally stand-offish Britons. The popularity in Britain of 'serio-comedies' implies that British critics and audiences prefer carefully rationed emotion and sincerity, within carefully defined situations and relationships. The occasional emotional climax or moment of truth is of course permissible, but feeling is not otherwise expected to keep intruding on normal life.

Wesker is aware of the importance of tone in communication – in his diary he records how a friend and translator of *The Merchant* had taken offence at one of his letters in a way that mystified him until he disentangled a certain sentence that was superficially dismissive: 'It was, without my voice, rude, insensitive, ungrateful'. The 'without my voice' is the crucial distinction – and he knew the same thing happened in interviews: 'What was self-deprecatory, because my tone of voice makes it so, will read as pompous on the page. I know it. I know it and always hate it and always swear I'll never do it again'. His own readings of his plays are invariably described as compelling and convincing, but as a dramatic writer he doesn't always keep within the tonal guidelines that actors and audiences can deal with.

A comment such as:

Perhaps I shouldn't be talking about this, but it seems as if the personality of the man has got in the way of the work. For reasons which I
really don't think I understand, I do seem to arouse hostilities and
irritations. (TQ 28 p. 5)

indicates that it is *not* 'the man' himself as a person that irritates
– it is his public persona. The public image of Arnold Wesker was
first established along with his new wave contemporaries, as
Michael Kustow only slightly exaggerates: 'Osborne the Misan-
thropic Growler, Arden the Marxist Bard, Wesker the Strident
Moralist'[2]. Not only is this image not true now – though its persistence is evident as play after play is greeted with amazement and
regret that it is not a re-vamp of *Roots* – but it was *never* true.
Even the early plays, even *Roots*, are far more complex and loaded
with qualifications and reservations than critical folk-memory
recalls. And the 'moral' (again, even of *Roots*) escaped a good
many reviewers at the time. A suitable epigraph for the critical
approach to Wesker's plays over the decades appeared in a *Scotsman* review of *Jerusalem*: 'This is nothing if not a didactic play,
yet the message is a little elusive'.

So the image of Wesker as a strident moralist, whose plays
therefore must have a strident moral, should be modified because
it simply gets in the way of what is actually there in the plays. It is
all part of Wesker's uncomfortable persona: behind the moralist
is seen what Richard Findlater described as 'this image of him as
an incorruptible, dedicated innocent at large', which in turn relates
to his embarrassingly un-English openness and lack of reserve.
Serious and sincere things can be said between individuals where
tone of voice establishes confidence, but in public speaking and
writing such seriousness and sincerity soon appear to be violating
the proper distance between strangers, and the audience or reader
recoils hastily to re-establish that distance, usually behind a barrier
of rejection or ridicule. In *Journey into Journalism* Wesker is told
by journalists as a self-evident fact that 'they have to represent
their story in caricature terms in order not to be caught being
serious, which would be an invitation to derision'; and he is
amazed: 'Why does seriousness invite derision?' (JJ p. 16). But on
the whole there is an inhibition against revealing what one is
serious about that makes it unlikely that 'a vulnerable man expos-

3

ing his confusions, wounds or despair' will evoke sympathy in the public at large. British cultural conventions resist change, but perhaps one should hope that Arnold Wesker will not change either.

In fact, like most people, Wesker *has* changed over the twenty-four years that have elapsed between *The Kitchen* and *Caritas*. The political position of the family in *Chicken Soup with Barley* was the position of Wesker's own family, and he explained his early political involvement in that context: 'I was a member of the Young Communist League for a short while, and coming from a Communist background one is always involved in political activity' (TW p. 80). He then joined the Zionist Youth Movement, however, 'and really I developed through that rather than through any political movement'. But by 1977 he was saying:

> I can only tell you simple things. Like it seems to me that what I've always been is a simple, old-fashioned humanist ... I think there are a lot of people who still feel that we are the socialists we always were, but that somehow we are out on a limb, floating in space, drawing inspiration from no one political movement, but from a long history of ... What? Rationalist action? Humanist philosophy? (TQ 28 p. 20)

The alienation from 'one political movement' – like his reservations about the trade unions' closed shop: 'I suppose I *am* worried about any organization which insists that everybody must belong to it. Though I fully realize the historical reasons for that' – stems from a very deep individualism, which perhaps runs counter to Wesker's 'social' image. And this profound individualism obviously relates to the way Wesker so often seems to be out of step with what is expected of a writer: his willingness to step out of line has been plain throughout his career. Other dramatists do this – John Osborne's explosions of rage, 'Damn you England', are a case in point – but Wesker has done it more and longer. By 1981 he was trying to avoid reading reviews 'because I felt so tired of all this', but ended up feeling guilty about not having read and replied where necessary 'because I always *have* hit back and I feel that I ought to go on hitting back'.

Curiously his willingness to step out of line is not entirely due to Wesker's family tradition of political protest. His mother was a fighter all her life, but in spite of this she 'was always fearful of my success, that I would draw attention to myself'. Nonetheless,

'My mother runs through all my work', and it is interesting how she always appears, reassuring or reprimanding, in even his most fragmentary childhood memories:

> I can remember making raids on Woolworth's with my friends and pinching the sweets from the cracks between the glasses, and playing truant from school to go to South Kensington to the museum, and one of the kids told his father who told my mother...
>
> I can remember playing Tin Can Copper, you know – walking backwards up the street with a tin can, while the others went into hiding. I can remember walking backwards for a long time, and then a car bumping into me. My mother took my trousers down to make sure there weren't any cuts on my backside. That was very embarrassing ... I can remember a copper walking me down the street, catching me at something I'd done, and I remember talking to him and persuading him not to tell my mother. And then I remember my aunts telling me that my grandmother had once looked at me and said: 'That boy, he'll either grow up to be a murderer or a very great man ...'³

His family moved away from the East End Fashion Street area when he was still quite young, but he recalls it with affection. On the other hand he has compared it with Shylock's Venetian ghetto: 'I felt very much in tune with Shylock, who lived in a ghetto. Now the East End is not a comparable ghetto, but it's a mentality'. The ambivalence may be between his generation's greater confidence and the older generation's 'fearful' mentality which he rejects.

The steps that made Wesker a dramatist are less obvious than for Osborne or Pinter, who were both actors before they started to write plays. The need to express himself, according to the amateur analysis of a Welsh uncle, arose from the rough patches of family life, not its closeness and sense of identity: the real-life uncle used the arguments given in a similar anecdote in the *Annie Wobbler* monologues:

> Your parents quarrelled and you loved them both and you've got conflict raging inside you ... Delusions of grandeur! *You* want to be a writer! You'll never be a writer. Not in a hundred years, never. But there it is, this drive in you to compensate ... Unhappy childhood, diminutive figure – classical!

The impulse to write in the first place (rather than to become a boxer, a tycoon or Napoleon, suggested by the Welsh uncle as alternatives) came 'because my brother-in-law wrote, and he was a hero for me, and I wanted to please him', (TW p. 80) but writing must also have been attractive because of Wesker's evident responsiveness to language. His mother had come from Transylvania, his father from Russia, and they spoke English as their common language at home – yiddish was not spoken unless by visitors. So the older generation spoke imperfect English with variations, and each with different variations, a background that focused attention on the problems of language – it couldn't be taken for granted. Wesker himself, as interviewers often comment, speaks without a trace of London or other accent, which he attributes to the influence of his elder sister Della who went to a good local school. In the film script that Wesker based on the Trilogy, Ronnie, who represents his own younger self asks his sister Ada (Della) 'Why do you talk posh and use long words?' and fifteen-year-old Ada retorts competently 'I don't talk posh. I talk properly. And Capitalists don't want the workers to use words properly because then they might think properly ... A Capitalist is someone who wants to keep the workers ignorant and illiterate so that he can manipulate them'. Apart from foreshadowing Wesker's later views on culture – no making a virtue out of the second rate –this relates to his interest in words as instruments of power as well as of communication.

The choice of drama seems to have come from an innate leaning towards the theatre; he had 'histrionic tendencies' and had cousins who were keen amateur actors and drew him into their productions. Arden, Osborne and Pinter all went to grammar or public schools, but Wesker like Ronnie failed his eleven-plus exam and went to Upton House school where he shone only in English (and was encouraged by his English teacher, like so many other writers). And he would have been an actor if he could; he passed the entrance audition for RADA, but didn't get a grant. So he went into a series of unskilled jobs before and after National Service: 'I decided I must take up a job, a trade, and if I was going to write I'd write anyway'. (TW p. 80) Having moved from unskilled to skilled work by training as a pastry-cook, he went to work in a restaurant in Paris, where he saved enough money to finance himself through a course at the London School of Film Technique – 'in its early days, when it really wasn't a school and we spent most of our time laying concrete floors' (TW p. 81). This seems an entirely characteristic transition: whether or not the pastry-cooking was an inevitable choice because of the traditional association of Jewish home, mother and food, it certainly reinforced Wesker's tendency to use food as an image for many kinds of human interaction. During *The Merchant* rehearsals John Dexter teased him about wanting to add a picnic to a scene – 'That will make FIVE meals in this play – I will write a book on 'Food in Wesker': *Calorific Wesker!*' And from *The Kitchen* onwards, the chicken soup, the chips have been succeeded by the strudel making in *The Four Seasons*, the sliced oranges in *Love Letters* and so on. 'Food is essential to all human activity', Wesker explains. 'When you invite people as guests, you touch them through food. And in the preparation of food there is a kind of ceremony, isn't there?' (TQ 28 p. 21). Perhaps it is natural that someone who instinctively turns to such an outward and visible demonstration of relationships should be drawn to drama: he has written several short stories, but has felt the need to recast certain of these in dramatic form, as plays or films. It was because of his wish so to recast his story 'Pools' that he first got to know Lindsay Anderson, whose film *Every Day Except Christmas* Wesker was queuing to see when he saw Anderson himself: 'I went up to him and asked him whether he would read a short story which I had written, which I thought could possibly be made into a film under the British Film Institute's experimental fund' (TW p. 81). And as Lindsay Anderson was working at the Royal Court Theatre, it was through him that Wesker began his own connection with the Court.

It was while going through this mixture of jobs that Wesker met his wife Dusty, then a waitress (her real name is Doreen; the story is that he told her her hair was like gold dust and Dusty she then became). Dusty came from Norfolk and had certain similarities with Beatie Bryant:

> Beatie Bryant in *Roots* is the daughter of farm labourers in Norfolk, and my wife is the daughter of farm labourers in Norfolk . . . What isn't obvious is what I choose to select and juxtapose and extend. I married my wife: Ronnie in *Roots* does not. (TW p. 79)

As he makes Dusty say in his autobiographical and unpublished *New Play* 'What about another play about me? . . . I was your best creation. Smashing girl, Beatie Bryant' – and everyone has agreed with her since. In the same play he describes her 'kneading dough, dicing meats, slicing carrots, whipping cream, dipping a finger here and there to taste – all done effortlessly, with enjoyment' for

7

the sixty people he has asked to a 'small' party; and the Wesker open-house home life reflects (perhaps on a slightly larger scale) the pattern of his mother's house. Again, in writing *The Merchant*, he drew on his own home life with Dusty in Bishop's Road, Hampstead, to create Shylock's:

> That household was written about *my* household, full of the children and their friends and my friends coming in and out, and the lunches and Sunday teas, and foreign visitors' teas. There's always an event in Bishop's Road and that's what I wanted to create on stage. A Ghetto full of life, 'a house never still'.

But on the other hand he is not dependent on other people for constant stimulus, but does a lot of his writing at his isolated cottage Blaendigeddi in Wales, following a solitary and austere regime. Dusty takes him there to be left until called for. He describes the stay he made there while working on *Caritas*:

> Drove with Dusty back to the crossroads and, as on other occasions, waved till she disappeared over the crest in the white Volvo. Gray, cold, blustery weather. She'd hoped for sun. 'It'll be hot tomorrow when I'm gone.'
> Walked back, strode, in my landscape again. Soul settled at once. Made my tinned fish salad, wept over the particularly strong onions, sliced my oranges and grapefruit, made my supply of coffee (weak this time, so's not to irritate the ulcer or whatever it is, though I'm feeling nothing now) and listened to the radio ... Extraordinary how I settle into the old routine at once and proceed to do what I could easily do in London but don't: slice my fruit, eat only the fish salad, garden, read and read, listen to the radio, type the *Merchant* diary.

The solitude can however be a disadvantage as, when having written two scenes of *The Merchant* and been stricken with bleak discouragement, he had no distraction or escape from his problem:

> And here I am, in the middle of the Black Mountains, isolated and alone with this dreadful discovery, this unbearable knowledge, and not even a vehicle into which I can throw my bags and leave.

But his attachment to the lonely Welsh landscape goes back to his early wartime stay as an evacuee in Wales (his aunts who also went still have traces of a Welsh accent), and to camping holidays in the Wye valley. This is the side of Wesker that enables him to present with conviction the anchoress's longing for solitary confinement in *Caritas*: the bustling 'house never still' is only half the story.

After Lindsay Anderson read *Chicken Soup* and 'wrote me this marvellous letter in which he said, yes, you really are a playwright, aren't you?' (TW p. 81), Wesker's success and reputation rose steadily until *Chips with Everything* in 1963. (He points out, however, that he has never been a big box-office draw – *Chips* was the only one of his plays that had a long run.) Not only had Wesker written *Chicken Soup* directly after seeing Osborne's *Look Back in Anger*, but he had a very conscious sense of being part of a new wave, more so perhaps than the other dramatists:

> We were all of us somehow absorbing the same kind of atmosphere: the war had been a formative part of our lives, followed by the hope of 1945, and the general decline from then on. So that we were the generation at the end of that decline, desperately wanting to find something, being tired of the pessimism and the mediocrity, and all the energy that was spent on being anti-Soviet and anti-Communist. (TW p. 83)

And he reacted indignantly to the suggestion that the new wave was just another phase; in a letter to the *New Statesman* he fiercely rejected this dismissive kind of attitude. For him the so-called working-class drama was not purely theatrical, but an expression of a social force: 'I see a vast link-up between the Universities and *Left Review* and Theatre Workshop, and the New Writers, and Suez, and "You never had it so good", and the Belgrade Theatre in Coventry'.[4] Like John Arden and Shelagh Delaney, he was an active supporter of the Campaign for Nuclear Disarmament and spent a month in Drake Hall open prison for participating in a civil disobedience demonstration in 1961.

The Centre Fortytwo project was a logical development from this standpoint. The purpose was to set up a centre that would act as a kind of pool of creative and performing talent that could be called on by communities, by-passing the culture-snobbery of the established metropolitan theatre-concert-gallery axis, particularly dominant in the West End. Though Wesker stressed later that the key words here were 'could be called on' and that nobody would force anything on to unwilling audiences, the accusation that he wanted to 'take Culture to the Masses' was still being tagged on to him by journalists fifteen years afterwards. The actual name of the project came from Resolution 42, carried unanimously by the Trades Union Congress in 1960:

> Congress recognized the importance of the arts in the life of the community, especially now when many unions are securing a shorter working week and greater leisure for their members. It notes that the trade union movement has participated to only a small extent in the direct promotion of plays, films, music, literature and other forms of expression, including those of value to its beliefs and principles. Congress considers that much more could be done, and accordingly requests the General Council to conduct a special examination and to make proposals to a future Congress to ensure a greater participation by the trade union movement in all cultural activities.[5]

Not the least revolutionary aspect was the proposal that the trade unions should finance the projected Centre – though this did not happen – to prevent commercial pressures subverting the whole project.

Centre Fortytwo had unexpectedly successful and hopeful beginnings. The first phase involved many like-minded artists, mainly belonging to a group that included Doris Lessing, John McGrath, Bernard Kops, Shelagh Delaney and many others who were also interested in bringing artist and public together without the interference of an intimidating or expensive organization. Wesker united the aims of this group with the trade union initiative and brought about a much more ambitious scheme than could have been mounted by the isolated little theatres or companies or movements that had been set up by enthusiasts with very limited funds and localized effect. And during this phase the nascent Centre Fortytwo flexed its muscles and established its name by putting on provincial arts festivals – the pioneering one at Wellingborough in 1961, six the next year in 1962. (These six festivals echo through the plays in the six golden cities planned in *Their Very Own and Golden City* and in the six bankrupt shops in *The Friends*.) It was Wesker's own insistence on nothing but the best, on first-class artistic quality (justified by the alacrity with which critics pounced on any organizational hassles), that was one motive for discontinuing these successful and promising festivals; another motive was, ominously, the debts they incurred.

The next phase involved the acquisition of the Roundhouse, then still an unconverted former engine shed in North London,

10

huge, circular and impressive, but inconvenient. More money was needed for the lease and to convert it into a playing space (though in 1964 Louis Minz and Alec Coleman gave Fortytwo the remaining sixteen-year lease of the building). Paradoxically the Roundhouse, the one solid survivor of the project, became something of a Frankenstein's monster to its owners, in that the problems of financing it and the successive fund-raising efforts overshadowed and wore out the original inspiration. The Arts Council gave a few tiny amounts; the TUC as a body did not offer any money, though individual unions and branches did contribute comparatively small sums. Centre Fortytwo then began to apply to industry and other private sources for money, and in the process of making the Roundhouse earn its own living, the businessmen who figured among its trustees effectively obliterated its original function. In 1970 Wesker formally dissolved the movement.

It is a fascinating episode, and several features stand out as illuminating Wesker's personality and plays. Both his impulse to harness the 'link up' of social forces because 'if nothing was done everything was going to be dismissed', and his anxiety to promote his ideas in the real world as well as in the theatre, relate to his ideal of the artist as a coherent 'whole man'. Artistic work should run parallel to social activities. Referring to his plays, he said:

> What must I do now? Is it enough to write them and help them on to a stage? How must I conduct the rest of my life? Have holidays in the South of France, amuse my friends at parties, rear children, vote, give talks on theatrical history? What can those works have meant to me if that is all I do once they are written? (FF p. 44)

The positive side of Wesker's character – unhampered by British cultural inhibitions – is evident in the move from talking to doing, and in the daring size of the project: 'We must stop thinking in terms of starting simply another little artistic project which makes a slight crack in the granite wall ... we have all too often failed in patchwork schemes ...' (FF p. 48). But side by side with this is the realism, almost pessimism, that threads through the plays:

> Somewhere inside me is a little voice nagging and whispering and warning that all the demands we make, all the Centre Fortytwos we may build, all the departments or ministries of culture we may create within the framework of a society can only be patchwork if that society remains at heart a capitalist society. (FF p. 79)

11

As reviewers regularly commented, all this was taking up a lot of energy that could have gone into writing plays. After the success of *Chips with Everything* the hiatus caused by Centre Fortytwo activities underlined the new direction that Wesker's writing was taking. The uncharacteristic experiment with poetic expressionism in *The Four Seasons* was unpopular, his next play *Golden City* was also little liked, and *The Friends* then suffered from the results of his unhappy British debut as director of his own play. Later he was to admit to an anxiety that 'a vicious circle will be created in which a play is attacked, fails, the next one isn't done, nor the next, there is a silence, Wesker isn't being produced, therefore what he next writes can't be any good, not done, longer silence . . .' On the other hand, the decline in his reputation as a new wave writer who was no longer writing the same sort of plays might have happened at this time in any case, as it did with his contemporaries Osborne and Arden. Because Centre Fortytwo was news intermittently over several years, Wesker's name grew familiar to non-playgoers and was kept in the public eye. But this reinforced the image of him as a campaigner for causes rather than as an artist. Looking back he said:

> The early days were marvellous and exciting of course, and when things were going well we all felt over the moon, involved in something special and unique. But when things began to go wrong it was very oppressive – that period was very unhappy. I don't think I regret it, except insofar as it created an image of me, which image has coloured the way in which my plays have been viewed and has done a lot of damage to the perspective on the plays.

After all the disillusion and bad feeling that this sort of disappointment seems to cause between colleagues and even friends, Wesker had given up the project reluctantly – as late as 1970 he was hoping that if *The Friends* was a success he might be able to salvage something of the original inspiration.

The seventies were difficult years for Wesker. He felt as though always trying to struggle out of a trough; bad luck dogged *The Old Ones* and *The Journalists* (described more fully in Part Two), and the star of the American production of *The Merchant*, Zero Mostel, died as the play began previewing. Successes, as of *The Wedding Feast* at Leeds or *Love Letters* at the National Theatre, did not generate an upward swing of interest in his work in Britain – but meanwhile his work was eagerly, even avidly siezed on by theatres all over the rest of the world: Japan and the Scandianavian countries showed a particular possessiveness about Wesker. And he continued to direct his plays abroad with a success startlingly in contrast with the ill-starred *Friends*. And in spite of the disillusion, rage and contempt that keep flaring up in diaries and letters, he would still reaffirm what he wrote about the need to assail again and again the foreknowledge of failure:

> I grow fearfully into middle age, wishing it could all happen again, and learn how to play it all by ear, as it comes, trusting the instinct, intelligence and experience rather than to knowledge I don't possess. I regret the passing of energies but hope still to surprise myself. Sometimes I resent the dream I've inherited, but then comes a time when I know for certain that the dream must always be restated; with all its naivety and simplicity, its helpless need to believe in man's goodness and reason, its longing for a kind of beauty in his city and nobility in his relationships. There will always be the decent and pragmatic men to talk it down and smile it away; those who, though wanting the dream, will find it not the time, yet; and those who will fight it with incomprehensible loathing, feeling that it challenges their miserable selves. So, the dream must be repeated – again and again and again – because it's the only measure, the only reminder we have that we could have made an oh-so-honier life for ourselves. And though we can't count on it coming in our lifetime (and perhaps, secretly, feel it never will) yet that dream must be lived out here and there, recorded, sung about and left lying about for the young. (SS p. 186)

2

Author, Directors, Critics

Wesker has acquired the reputation of touchiness towards directors and critics – an attitude that is absolutely consistent with his
beliefs about his own work, and with his views on the relationship
of all writers to their work. The London premieres of his first five
plays were at the Royal Court Theatre, directed by John Dexter
and most of them designed by Jocelyn Herbert. All but *Chips with
Everything*, however, were first tried out at the Belgrade Theatre
Coventry, as Wesker stresses:

> I dwell upon the Court's retreats and hesitations because it seems to me
> ... that their real courage, as far as my work is concerned, lay in their
> continuing to present it even when they seemed not to comprehend its
> success. The peak, of course, was the presentation of the entire *Trilogy*
> in the summer of 1960. But their mistrust of my work continued. They
> turned down *Chips with Everything* and only agreed to mount it
> after a commercial impresario, Bob Swash, persuaded them to share
> costs.[1]

What the Royal Court had given, Wesker said, was a feeling of
working 'as part of a team', which reinforced his reluctance to
hand over his script for package-deal production by some unknown agency. The Royal Court's misgivings about the plays were
something he was to encounter over and over again, as he protested
later in a letter to Peter Hall:

> Time and time again I've been vindicated, and still I'm not trusted.
> When does trust in me begin to operate instead of trust in you? Your
> record is as pitted or glittering as mine. Dexter, though perceptive
> about the *Trilogy* and *Chips* when the Court were wrong (yes, they also
> turned down *Chips* at first) was himself wrong in his advice to Bill
> Gaskill over the *Golden City*. *I've* make *that* work. Just as perhaps you
> were wrong about *The Wedding Feast* – I've seen that work in two
> cities now – and perhaps wrong about *The Journalists* which, after that
> reading, I *know* works. Why is that it takes so long for experienced
> theatre people to – I don't know what – to *hear* the plays? I hear them.
> Clearly. Sharply. And they're vibrant while most theatre here is effi-
> ciently life-less.

Balancing his often repeated statement that the rehearsal period of the first production is the final draft of a play is his absolute conviction that the play's essential existence is as it is conceived in the playwright's mind. In a letter to John Madden who first directed *Caritas* Wesker praised the parts which had come out to his satisfaction as 'sung almost entirely as I heard it in my head'. This of course includes not only the words of the dialogue but mood, rhythm and so on:

> Most people at work in the theatre would agree that it is neither possible nor desirable to write in the stage directions for every shift of limb, flick of eye or intonation of voice, but I'm very conscious of the physical relationships of characters to one another, of particular actions while speaking, of the emotive effect of colours and textures, the visual impact of structures, the choreography of movement, the speed of delivery. (P & P Feb. 1974)

And it is obviously frustrating that this totality is not conveyed by a simple reading of the script, as it hardly can be. Likewise frustrating is the realization that a writer cannot stop a director presenting his play differently from that first private vision. Wesker evolved an argument for a writer's having the right to direct the *first* production of his plays himself, asserting that 'there is no mystique inherent in the craft of directing, the craft can be learnt. The learning may not make a great director but *it can be learnt*'.

> A new dimension, it is true, can be brought to the production of a play by a director. But are all *new* dimensions inevitably *good* dimensions? There does exist the danger of an *incorrect* dimension. Perhaps the phrase 'new dimension' belongs more to the *often* performed play which is so familiar to theatregoers that a 'new dimension' can bring fresh light on the play's meaning, whereas a *new* play on its first exposure should be allowed to emerge with the *author's* concept of its dimensions – warts and all! (P & P Feb. 1974)

The concept of the original, authentic, essential version of the play existing in the writer's head is notoriously Pirandellian, and Wesker quotes Margaret Drabble on the greater control enjoyed by the novelist with an example that recalls the Actors' misrepresentation of the Characters in *Six Characters in Search of an Author*. Drabble:

> No, I don't ever want to write plays. What? Put in a stage direction for a certain kind of yellow hat to be worn, one that's absolutely represen-

tative of the character's personality and you can be sure they'll get the wrong bloody colour if they bother to get a hat at all because the actress is allergic to things on her head or something! Give me prose every time where the reader reads exactly what I've written, whether I'm making mistakes or not ... at least they're my mistakes. (P & P Feb. 1974)

And on this kind of alteration Wesker also quotes Harold Pinter, who had publicly objected to an Italian production of his *Old Times* directed by Luchino Visconti. Pinter:

It is certainly an inventive production. Signor Visconti has in fact invented a new play, where major, significant and quite crucial pieces of action are introduced into a play by the director without consultations with the author ... Let me remind you that a play is not public property. It belongs to its author under the international law of copyright. (P & P Feb. 1974)

So Wesker's relationship with his directors can have its tense periods:

You have no idea how despairingly impotent one feels when another has the control of one's play; especially for a writer like myself who also feels one should give the director as much breathing space as possible. My loyalty is split between my play and my director. Invariably the play suffers. Other writers scream and create scenes. I'm very anxious to maintain calm for everyone and so I leave things till the last moment by which time it's too late, always imaging the director is going to do something, but he doesn't!

Wesker's most important relationship has been with John Dexter, who shares Wesker's working-class background and remembers their first meeting on a CND march from Aldermaston. Dexter:

Marching convulsed me with embarrassment. I played games with myself, trying to pretend I was on my own. The singing and chanting embarrassed me, and the little dark chap on my right embarrassed me more than anything else. For almost an hour he was a constant irritation to me before we spoke; he seemed so at home with the banner in his hand, rain dripping down his face, and I felt such an inadequate and self-satisfied nit. Whilst drying out later in the afternoon, we discovered that I had just read his play *Chicken Soup with Barley* which had been sent to the Court by Lindsay Anderson. (P&P April 1962)

Dexter stayed with the Weskers at their home for some time, but

16

their friends and life-styles were and remain quite different. In a double interview with Ronald Hayman in 1972 they explained

DEXTER: We're terribly . . .

WESKER: Dissimilar.

DEXTER: I suppose we see each other in working relations about as much as Morecambe and Wise, and out of it about as little.

WESKER: That's terrible. We'll become known as the Morecambe and Wise of theatre.

DEXTER: I don't mind being compared with the best.[2]

For Wesker, attending and participating in rehearsals was the next best thing to directing himself. The considerable sympathy and common experience of the two men at best brought out the potential 'perfect' performance of the plays, and at worst came under strain when their priorities for the plays pulled in different directions. Dexter's contribution to the plays he directed has been substantial at times, though difficult for them to remember afterwards:

WESKER: In the service of *The Kitchen* I'd indicated [the action] in the script and written a little bit of it, but it wasn't enough, so when John came to do it, the shape of the service, the number of orders that had to be called out in order to make that service work, is the result of John's building up of that passage. The dance in *Roots* is indicated in the script and the coke-stealing episode [in *Chips with Everything*].

DEXTER: Precisely clear. It couldn't be done any other way. But Arnold had always seen them going into the coke. I'd always seen the coke where the audience was. Everything else was written into it completely. All the physical movements are firmly indicated. Even the tempi.[3]

More substantially, Dexter had looked at the first draft of *The Kitchen* and said 'It needs a middle section. I don't care what it is, except that it's got to be quiet. Now go away and write it' and in *The Old Ones* he'd objected to the three members of the younger generation being all men. Wesker:

And John first of all said 'I'd like one of them to be a girl just simply for the sound of it. To have a female voice'. But second he said 'All you've written here belongs to a female and not to a male'. Which threw up some interesting points.[4]

No director is going to have totally identical views on a play to those of its author, however, and problems arose when authenticity conflicted with acceptability. There was more than one hiatus in the Wesker-Dexter relationship; Dexter had not liked Wesker's sixth and seventh plays, and with the eighth, *The Friends*, Wesker was seeking to avoid directorial conflict by directing himself. (Ironically, in the event, his conflicts with the actors were worse.) With *The Old Ones* Dexter resumed the relationship.

Wesker's strong feeling for his plays appears in the sexual and family imagery he uses of them; later he was to refer to the misuse of a writer's plays as 'rape', and during *The Old Ones* rehearsals he said:

> WESKER: Starting work with a director on a play is a bit like watching a young man woo your daughter.
> DEXTER: Really?
> WESKER: You watch him handle her moods and rhythms and you think 'Christ! He's being a bit clumsy'. So you shut up and sit back and watch her teach him a bit about herself, and you watch him influence her.[5]

And Dexter agreed at least with the 'sit back and shut up' role of the author: 'You have to find out how to screw the daughter for yourself. No one else can woo Cinderella into a glass slipper for you.'

The tensions come to a head before the emotional release of the first night. Of *The Old Ones* Wesker wrote in an article for *The Guardian*:

> Rehearsals are amongst the happiest I've known. But the approach of first night brings with it yet another set of tensions. It's nearing the moment when that 'umbilical cord' must be broken. The play is no longer in my hands but entrusted to others. I can bear that: what I can't bear is being made to feel the play is no longer mine, treated like a stranger in my own house.[6]

He added: 'I want to talk, to feel I still belong'. He suspected Dexter of avoiding him: 'The director ceases to communicate. There's no reason. There have been no quarrels. Some areas of disagreement in production remain, but so what! Old resentments smoulder'. In fact Dexter was just going down with a painful back injury (he had to spend the last few days of rehearsal directing from a makeshift bed). Wesker: 'I phone him. "I've not been evading you", he says; "I've just had this pain and left quickly." So! It's my paranoia.' Wesker concluded the article:

From hour to hour moods and relationships change, mercurially. If changes don't take place it's not because of intransigence but because – because – because of what? At this late stage I can't tell. I'm now schizoid. One of me is calm and full of trust, admiration and faith; that me is visible. The other is anguished, resentful, full of dreads – and hidden.[7]

The *Guardian* article was resented by Dexter as being very far from the best way of keeping dreads and dissention hidden. The veiled threat suggested in another paragraph ('Fortunately there are no major disagreements – only subtle ones – if it were otherwise I'd call on every weapon to protect the play, even the law') probably didn't help either. And then Dexter made a sudden change of the final tableau against Wesker's wishes, when it was too late to change it back, which in turn alienated Wesker. Yet, just as they had been reconciled to put the play on in the first place, the coolness and loss of contact was to be overcome again, and communication re-established, though Dexter's words in 1962 were perhaps over-optimistic:

The sustained friendship which has survived five years of intensive collaboration is for me the most valued part of whatever we may have achieved. During this time, our sometimes acrimonious rows have been always productive and professional, never personal. We seem able to cancel out each other's capacity for self-indulgence. (P & P April 1962)

Both men's careers went on different courses after these early Royal Court days, but they came together again with the American production of *The Merchant*. And when Wesker tried to explain Shylock in terms of his own character, Dexter unexpectedly expressed similar involvement with the story. Wesker:

Then John wanted to talk about Antonio and Shylock in the light of his and my relationship. He said how much he identified with Antonio as the Christian being recieved into the Wesker house. He had this sharp memory of Dusty and me taking him in to our flat in Clapton Common at a difficult time in his career and that's why he'd responded to the Antonio-Shylock relationship. It had not occurred to me.

So, renewed friendly relations followed the tension and coolness with which rehearsals of *The Merchant* ended – this time occasioned by the cuts to the play. Wesker simply says 'John is a very complex personality'.

Of other directors, Wesker recalls the one who 'abstracted every-thing so that the sets looked like a boutique's designs for modern living' – this was for *Chips*! – and, for *The Four Seasons* in Belgium one who 'had a concept of the play in which if my text didn't fit he cut out whole sections of it'. Typically he explodes 'Directors! What *they* can't make work they imagine doesn't'. At least in foreign countries, he can say, he has 'been fortunate enough to have slowly commanded the right (and the technique) to control my own work'.

Then there is what he calls 'the final hazard of the 'after-math commentator'. Wesker's willingness to 'hit back' at the commen-tators is consistent with his readiness for 'battles' on all fronts: it is also consistent with his rejection of British behavioural conven-tions – decent reserve, gentlemanly silence. He does not see silence in the face of criticism as gentlemanly at all. The 'intolerable implication of silence' is that the writer is a 'puppy' who should 'dumbly accept kicks'. He is quite aware that the convention is to assume an appearance of being above the struggle, but his charac-ter demands that he involve himself:

> All such defences involve apparent indignity but the alternative of silence is not in my nature and I hope sufficient charity exists, still, to permit me a loyalty to that. (TQ 2 p. 30)

So he writes various detailed replies to critics, individually and *en masse*. After *The Friends* his article 'Casual Condemnations' spe-cified several failings on the part of the critics, including 'imagining their early opinions had applauded when in fact they had been derisive or indifferent', and 'sacrificing fact to feeble humour' and 'failure to listen to the play'. His suggestion that overnight reviews should be descriptive and tentative, and that serious criticism should have a longer period for digestion and well-supported analysis, is not unacceptable to many critics – and this kind of responsible criticism would require a reading of the text as well. Conscientious critics like Irving Wardle of *The Times* read texts of revivals of classic plays as a matter of course; and Wesker sends round a text of his plays to critics, but not all of them take advantage of this.

The difference of opinion here is between Wesker's view, that criticism must never be casual, because in practice 'a review, by attracting (or not attracting) a live audience, ensures (or does not ensure) a livelihood (TQ 2. 17), and because ethically it is wrong 'irresponsibly' to draw conclusions 'in hours about work that has taken years to accumulate or create'; and the opposite idea that a play must make its impact clearly then and there, within the performance time, because this is the experience the audience receives. Thus Harold Hobson voiced the usual reservation about reading a new play 'since I like to come to a play as to an entirely fresh experience'. Yet if it is accepted that texts of established plays can be read, the principle rather oddly ends by handicapping the new play as against the revival. One could argue that the critic is after all *not* merely a member of the audience but is expected to add something of value to the average perception of the play. And not all good plays clear the 'immediate impact' hurdle effortlessly – even twenty years on the majority of newcomers to Arden's *Serjeant Musgrave's Dance* find its 'message' quite baffling, yet they would not therefore deny it its place as 'modern classic'.

Wesker's replied to critics of his next play, *The Old Ones*, were more individual – indeed more personal. He accused John Russell Taylor of writing a 'transparently revengeful review' (P&P November 1972) to pay him back for the 'Casual Condemnations' article, and went on to attack Taylor's style, logic, assumptions and understanding. John Russell Taylor wrote 'more in sorrow than in anger' his own reply in the same issue, beginning 'I'm sorry Arnold Wesker takes every breath of adverse criticism so personally . . .' He denied vindictiveness, and argued that the hesitations of his style were often in aid of giving Wesker the benefit of the doubts in his own mind. Wesker has expressed surprise at the rudeness of critics in print, far beyond what they would dream of saying to a writer's face, but he is not mealy-mouthed himself when it comes to his counterblasts. Harold Hobson had spent a third of his review of *The Old Ones* objecting to the lack of sensitivity with which Wesker makes Manny 'show the audience his bottom during the evocation of a religious ceremony of his own faith', and another third on Wesker's paranoia – as 'a necessarily unpalatable effort to shock him into abandoning his obsession that he is a man treated with universal injustice'. Wesker replied with an Open Letter (which was too late to appear in the *Sunday Times*, Hobson's paper, and which he gave to be auctioned in aid of Oxfam: it was later printed in *Drama* no. 107). In it he calls the review 'a revealing and pompous piece of cretiny', and asserts 'You're not the maker of theatrical rules and regulations, you're only a reviewer, and a very lazy one at that'. Asking 'have you thought of retiring?' (Harold Hobson was then sixty-eight) he concludes the letter

> Retire! It can't be all that pleasant to devote a whole life-time to earning a living, scavenger-like, from the dead flesh of a living literature which you slaughter. You've made your contributions to the history of theatre journalism. Don't wait for senility to set in and spoil it all.
>
> And if you think I'm being rude – my God! You're right! You cannot claim the unilateral right to rudeness and hide behind your function without expecting someone to say something. So, though by now I've learnt that you're in a position to help make or break a serious play (only in this country, thank heavens!) yet I feel I've nothing more to lose if I don't take the imbecilities of a cretinue of critics lying down.

Hobson himself had recourse to dignified silence – 'If anything that could be said would calm Mr. Wesker's fears, or lessen his misery I would gladly say it', he said, declining the offer of reply in *Drama*.

But apart from these public statements, Wesker has also written letters to individual critics. Benedict Nightingale's review of *Caritas* in the *New Statesman* began by saying that, in his files – between a postcard from John Osborne

> warning me 'it might be healthier to keep away from downtown Chichester', and the letter from Peter Nichols congratulating himself on having refrained from murdering me after my review of *Privates on Parade* – is a ratty piece of orange paper plastered with the hectically-typed thoughts of Arnold Wesker.

This critical letter on orange paper was about *Love Letters on Blue Paper*, in which Nightingale called Wesker 'a natural optimist', and in reply Wesker claimed that the optimism was actually 'defiance':

> People fail, make horrendous mistakes in their lives, are betrayed, grow to dislike themselves, grow old, face death and yet – it always amazes me, they go on, and often with grace.

Quoting this, Nightingale was not won over: it was 'ringing stuff' but he didn't think it was 'an adequate recipe for a socialist playwright'. So there we are. Wesker concluded his letter 'God knows why I write to you of all the critics. I suppose it's because

Arnold Wesker. *Above:* in his study in London. *Below:* with Elizabeth Spriggs rehearsing *Love Letters on Blue Paper*, National Theatre, 1978.

Above: The Kitchen, English Stage Company, 1961.
Below: Chicken Soup With Barley, Shaw Theatre, 1978.

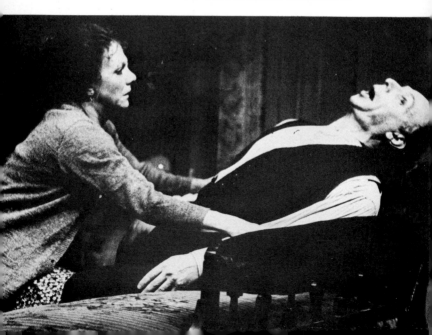

I detect some intelligent thoughtfulness behind all the careless nonsense with which you try to hide it'. He did nonetheless write to other critics, not always with such alienating effect. David Nathan in the *Jewish Chronicle* reviewing the 1978 revival of the Trilogy disliked Ronnie's 'standing on a table, his arms outstretched . . . Come to think of it, a lot of Wesker's characters jump about on the furniture'. Wesker replied aggressively 'I know you don't think the *Jewish Chronicle* is very important – at least that's how it comes over in your column – but for your own self respect you shouldn't write reviews the way you did the one on *Jerusalem*' and went on to say that Ronnie stood on a chair, not a table, once only, and asked just what other furniture-jumping took place? David Nathan did not take refuge in dignified silence, nor file the letter away for further reference, but replied with equal vigour that he was in fact Assistant Editor of the *Jewish Chronicle* and that Beatie Bryant stood on a table or chair in *Roots*, and added 'I'm sorry, too, that you do not like my joke, but there are a few jokes of yours that I do not care for, and a sense of humour is a notoriously difficult thing to share'. Wesker then came back 'unrepentant since I meant to hurt' and argued that one Beatie was not 'a lot' of characters. But later the same year when, in the course of reviewing *The Merchant*, Nathan commented on the 'marvellously vigorous' scene in which Shylock is 'aglow – like the young Ronnie in Wesker's early plays (even to the extent of jumping on a chair in his excitement)', Wesker wrote to him:

> Do you know I've only just received a copy of your review of *The Merchant*. And since I've picked on you twice to complain I feel I must pick on you at least once to say 'thank you' . . .
>
> By the way, the standing on the chair was not in my script (Ronnie's doing so was), but when David Swift wanted to do it, or perhaps it was the director, I smiled and let them keep it in thinking 'This move is for David Nathan'!

As in Dexter's early assessment, the disagreement could be professional and not personal – and yet Wesker's consciousness that the survival of his long-prepared work and his income from it depended on the critics made his reaction to casual jokiness, when destructive, extremely strong. If the director's relationship to the play is like a young man wooing your daughter, then, as Wesker's exclamation over the New York reviews of *The Mer-*

chant suggests – 'the reviews have murdered the play's life' – then hostile and dismissive critics must seem like the beloved daughter's assassins. Obviously Wesker is not exceptional in his bitter resentment of critics in general, as Benedict Nightingale's reference to his dramatists' correspondence indicates – can they all be dismissed as unsportsmanlike? – but he is exceptional in tossing dignity aside and protesting again and again.

3

The Kitchen

The Kitchen was, in its original one-act version, Wesker's very first play, which he wrote 'suddenly' for the Observer play competition of 1957, though it was not produced until after *Chicken Soup* and *Roots*. It is one of his cyclical plays: its time span (one day) is complete in itself and one can imagine it being infinitely repeated, like the eight week training period of the airmen in *Chips*, or the one year love affair in *The Four Seasons*. So, the play gives us a typical day in the life of a big restaurant kitchen, with the eternal pressures and irritations, the quarrels and relaxation and so on – only the climax, in which a maddened cook sabotages the gas supply, is perhaps not quite an everyday occurence. Already themes appear that are to preoccupy the author for the next decade; Wesker's introduction says, with what he was later to call 'youthful bravado',

> The world might have been a stage for Shakespeare, but to me it is a kitchen: where people come and go and cannot stay long enough to understand each other, and friendships, loves, and enmities are forgotten as quickly as they are made. (*II* 9)

First there is the belief that people are shaped, or perhaps more accurately in this case, stunted, by their environment, and by extension, by their society. Then there is the related concern for roots – properly established relationships, involvement in work – and modern man's lack of them.

Because the environment is important in itself, much of the play simply presents what is involved in the slow beginning of work in the morning, the frantic lunch service (this is a big place serving two thousand customers a day), the lull of the off-duty afternoon period, and the equally frantic evening service. Against this background, the individual drama of the main character, a young German cook, Peter, pursues its similarly monotonous course of rows and reconciliations with his workmates, and rows and reconciliations with his married girlfriend Monique, a waitress. Finally, an exceptionally definitive rebuff by Monique drives him to the point of explosion; he seizes an axe and by severing the main gas pipe to the ovens brings the kitchen to a standstill.

A whole play consisting of typical cooking, floor-sweeping and so forth, relieved only by the one climax at the end, seemed painfully lacking in dramatic stiffening in 1961: the raw content was fascinating, but as a play it 'wanted art'. *The Times* critic complained that 'the slice-of-life pictures somehow do not bite on the mind of the spectator. They badly need a story to lift them into stage significance'. This of course was ten years before the Royal Court had great success with David Storey's detailed genre pieces, such as *The Contractor* and *The Changing Room*, with their almost hypnotically authentic recreation of certain life-styles. Though the lack of a 'strong' plot-line was to to be a perennial complaint against Wesker, the more sophisticated post-Storey critics would be more likely to question whether the injection of dramatic climax was really necessary, and indeed it came too late for some of the original audience. 'This documentary – it cannot be called a play' said the *Punch* critic, 'has not sufficient story to knit the characters dramatically', while the 'ending is pure melodrama, for which we are unprepared'. And T. C. Worsley analysed the effect further: 'it is the sort of ending which is theatrically effective rather than entirely satisfying. It holds us while we are in the theatre, but when we come out and reflect on it, it doesn't seem to add up quite so well'.

Internally, however, the text prepares quite adequately for the violent conclusion; the first topic of conversation as the cooks arrive is how Peter escaped with a black eye from threatened attack only the previous evening, and one of the play's main theses, the environmental argument, is that the kitchen turns people into pigs.

> DIMITRI: They all wanted to fight. Listen, you put a man in the plate room all day, he's got dishes to make clean and stinking bins to take away and floors to sweep, what else there is for him to do – he wants to fight. He got to show he is a man someway. So – blame him. (*II* 20)

And the play recognizes, as T. C. Worsley pointed out, that in real life a violent gesture effects nothing: 'the world doesn't stop for such'. Peter is what Esther in a later play *The Friends* defines as a rebel, merely destructive (as opposed to a constructive revolu-

26

tionary): 'Men are only ever rebels, their angers are negative, tiny' (*III* 106). As Peter says himself '– why do you grumble about this kitchen? What about the offices and factories?' (*I* 48). Taking an axe to Marango's gas pipes is merely a tiny gesture. But in human, non-symbolic terms, the sheer pressure of work, increasing naturally to top speed, almost demands an explosion, a breaking point, and for some in the audience this outburst came as something of a relief; the *Queen* critic defended its culminative effect:

> The melodrama is totally motivated, and I was stunned by the way Robert Stephens played it: not upstage and in a fury, as before, but downstage, five feet from the stalls, and in a moment of curious practical calm.

The sense of pressure, like the creation of interest in kitchen routines, depends heavily on the director. The *Sunday Times* critic testified to this from his own experience:

> When I saw it at a National Union of Students–Sunday Times Festival eighteen months ago I did not recognize its merits. It was neither badly acted nor badly directed. But its performance then did not have the sleight-of-hand efficiency in detail of John Dexter's production at the Court, nor its strong controlled musical flow.

Wesker's introduction says that in such a restaurant, 'the quality of the food here is not so important as the speed with which it is served' (*II* 9) and so all the cooks must be seen to be doing something purposeful all the time. As Dexter was to point out, Wesker's notes for the director give *general* activities for waitresses, porters, etc., and a list of dishes and related cooking processes for each cook – for instance, Peter is allotted 'Mixed fish – sauce. Cod meuniere – boiled potatoes. Boiled turbot – sauce hollandaise. Beat egg yellows on slow heat; add melted margarine for sauce hollandaise. This takes a long time. Slice cod and turbot into portions. Slice lemons for garniture'; what is important is that 'Each person has his own particular job. We glance in upon him, high-lighting as it were the individual. But though we may watch just one or a group of people, the rest of the kitchen staff does not. They work on'. This highlighting is a problem for the director, particularly as the oppressive, head-aching roar of the ovens 'is a noise that will stay with us to the end' (*II* 15) and 'There will be this continuous battle between the dialogue and the noise of the

27

ovens. The producer must work out his own balance' (*II* 15). Bamber Gascoigne had also seen the student production, and pinpointed the major difficulties as the absence of real food and consequent need to mime its preparation, and the audibility of dialogue.

I have seen elsewhere a production of *The Kitchen* in which the director failed to master these two difficulties, and it seemed a play of unparalleled incompetence. At the Court Wesker is lucky in his director. John Dexter conducts the whirlwind in a well-controlled *accelerando*, coaxes such good miming out of his cooks that the lack of edibles becomes food for art, and even goes some way towards solving the one-conversation-at-a-time problem. The only free space in his kitchen is at the very front of the stage. This is where the staff eat; this is where they come if they want to talk. Anyone speaking to them from the back of the kitchen has to shout above the roar of the ovens. Ordinary chat at the back of the kitchen can therefore be carried on on unheard.

There is in fact a lot of legitimate movement built into the cooks' duties – collecting things from the vegetable room or cold cupboard and so on – so there are many opportunities for encounters downstage. John Dexter's direction dazzled the audience: 'Like some superb juggler', described Bernard Levin, 'he keeps a huge cast weaving, reacting, colliding, in a faultless choreography. (There are 23 people on the stage simultaneously at one point, all of them acting and most of them talking.)' And Robert Muller agreed that 'the piece is splendidly visual: the white-hatted polyglot cooks dart about between the stoves and tables; we are made aware of the heat, the exasperation, the stealing, the flirtations ...'. Not only was it visual: 'Not a scrap of food is actually used on the stage. Yet so completely persuasive are both dramatist and producer that we can almost smell the stench'.

Ideally the play should be performed without a break so that the rest-period scene can cut abruptly across the high-speed lunch service, a peak of activity that impressed Kenneth Tynan more than the final curtain: 'John Dexter's direction is flawless, rising at the end of the first half to a climatic lunch-hour frenzy that is the fullest theatrical expression I have seen of the laws of supply and demand'. This particular sequence drew Peter Roberts's attention to the theatrical 'juggler' aspect of the direction: 'rejecting a merely realistic show', John Dexter produces a 'virtuoso display' and 'in the swirling close of the first part the movements pass on beyond

28

the naturalistic to the stylized. It is a very beautiful blending of two approaches'. Alan Brien was another who gave Dexter the credit for 'convincing us that we are watching absolute naturalism while imposing on his almost universally brilliant cast of 30 a style of highly individual formalism'. But a glance at the stage directions shows that Wesker must share this credit since the 'highly individual formalism' is written into the overall direction of the scene: 'The whole tempo of work is speeded up suddenly' for the last sequence.

This naturalism/expressionism diagnosis is not just an academic question but has a real bearing on the success of different productions. In an unpublished lecture, 'The Nature of Development', Wesker extends the usual concept of the artist presenting his raw material (life, truth, reality) in one of a variety of ways – naturalistic, absurdist, symbolist or whatever – by dividing up the raw material also into categories 'what is absurd in reality', or 'what is paradoxical in reality', so that

> the artist is dealing with what is absurd in reality in a naturalistic form – as Pinter sometimes does, or he's dealing with naturalistic aspects of reality in an absurd form which is what I think is happening in Beckett's *Godot*.

So labelling of this kind should not be as crude and divisive as it tended to be in the case of these early plays:

> I wanted it fully appreciated that I shared, in common with *all* artists, the function of exploring reality. It means nothing to think of my plays and stories as social realism – a term I've always resented because it blinded people to those other elements in my work I'd always hoped would be recognised: the paradoxical, the lyrical, the absurd, the ironic, musical, farcical and so on; all the elements united, as Ruskin says, 'in due place and measure'.

The element of symbolism got rather more than its due place and measure, perhaps; by 1963 Wesker was saying

> in *The Kitchen* I would not, if I were writing the play now, make Dimitri *say* that the kitchen is like the whole world. It's not that I've changed my mind about what I was trying to say in those plays; it's just that I think now I would say them in a different way ...

eschewing specifically 'bald verbal statements', and in revising the play he did cut out this and similar statements. It was the peaceful off-duty scene that provoked several accusations of overstatement and pedagogy. Dimitri does in fact echo his author's words in the introduction: 'Is different anywhere else? People come and people go, big excitement, big noise ... In the end, who do you know?' (*II* 47) Not only the baldness, but the clarity and consciousness in this kitchen porter are unexpected, and Peter's rejoinder, 'You're a very intelligent boy, Dimitri', sounds slightly defensive on the part of the playwright. Paul, the most articulate and thoughtful of the cooks, expands on the problem of knowing people:

> Listen Peter – I'll tell you something. I'm going to be honest with you. You don't mind if I'm honest – Right! I'm going to be honest with you. I don't like you. Now wait a minute, let me finish. I don't like you! You bully, you're jealous, you go mad with your work, you always quarrel. All right! But now it's quiet, the ovens are low, the work has stopped for a little and now I'm getting to know you. I still think you're a pig only now – not so much of a pig. (*II* 51)

And he illustrates the way that pressurized people behave like pigs with an anecdote about his neighbour, a bus driver, whom Paul had sympathized with during a busman's strike, but who made no effort to return this sympathy when Paul went on a big Peace March

> Now I don't want him to say I'm right, I don't want him to agree with what I did, but what makes me so sick with terror is that he didn't stop to think that this man helped me in my cause so maybe, only *maybe*, there's something in his cause, I'll talk about it. No! The buses were held up so drop a bomb, he says, on the lot! And you should have seen the hate in his eyes, as if I'd murdered his child. Like an animal he looked. And the horror is this – that there's a wall, a big wall between me and millions of people like him. And I think – where will it end? What do you do about it? And I look around me, at the kitchen, at the factories, at the enormous bloody buildings going up with all these offices and all those people in them and I think Christ! I think Christ, Christ, Christ! (*II* 52)

But, as Wesker points out later 'that's the longest and only monologue there is in the play'; in commenting on the situation this was as far as he could allow his characters to go, between the two extremes of simple formulations, and unconvincing perceptiveness, because 'there is no one around with a mind or imagination

30

of any quality to shape the action at a more profound level'. It is the same problem that exercised audiences of *Roots* (or of the early plays of Pinter), in that demonstrating the failure of communication by showing characters failing to communicate can also fail to communicate with the audience. In *The Kitchen* it is the failure of the *will* to communicate, rather than verbal breakdown, that is dividing the kitchen workers against each other, and as long as no one has to discuss the failure, the action shows it well enough. Amongst the lesser characters Alfredo is 'a typical cook in that he will help nobody and will accept no help; nor will he impart his knowledge'; likewise, we see the Chef refuse to answer queries about whether the menu should say plaice or sole, Margolis the porter won't clean a strainer, and Peter while actually helping the new chef Kevin won't let him borrow his cutting board just for a minute: 'Oh no, no, no, my friend, the plate room, the plate room, in the plate room you'll find them'. As the stage direction comments, 'In the kitchen it is each man for himself now' (*II* 45) The separation of the cooks is the more evident because of the great range of nationalities in the kitchen. Not only do misunderstandings arise because of an imperfect grasp of English, but nationality provides an insult ready to hand when quarrels flare up – 'lousy Cypro', 'bloody German bastard'. The sporadic nationalism, or racism, is just another aspect of the same refusal to communicate that divides the bus driver from the peace marcher.

However, the members of this 'United Nations', as Dimitri puts it, during the peaceful period when a little understanding develops, tentatively confide their dreams of a better life – dreams that range from a workshop to a million dollars; but Peter, who initiated the 'dream competition', can't produce a single dream himself. Later, when taxed with this, he replies sadly 'I can't dream in a kitchen' (*II* 61). Now, curiously, although the conversation during this scene was accused of over-explicitness, preaching and so on, it had a positive and consoling effect on some of the audience; the *Sunday Times* liked the 'long slow movement of considerable beauty, in which the dreams, the desires, the aspirations of mankind are articulated with melancholy and with hope'; and Gareth Lloyd Evans who *dis*liked the whole 'formless, noisy, tasteless, quasi-realism' of the play, assumed that 'the message is that we can all dream, even if we have to live in a hotel kitchen', which is more or less the opposite of what Peter at least is saying.

Because they end with Peter's *inability* to dream, the dreams surely should underline, rather than compensate for, the kitchen's real-life stunting effect – yet in John Dexter's production Robert Stephens as Peter built an archway of saucepans, a concrete dream, a construct that contradicted his verbally sterile imagination. This had considerable impact (and was incorporated into the revised text), as V. S. Pritchett described it:

> The moment when he builds his triumphal arch of bins and saucepans on the stoves and goosesteps under them was exquisite: it had an absurdity that was at once touching, noble and frightening. One didn't know whether to laugh or cry, invoke Heine or call the police.

This was perhaps the equivalent in terms of action of making Dimitri a little bit too analytic: too much constructiveness here, and the problems of the play will seem to be on the verge of solution, the effect being simple and propagandist; on the other hand, too much realistic apathy and resistance to change, and the audience has the impression that the slice of life is immutable and inevitable, the message one of despair. These are the Scylla and Charybdis of misinterpretation to which several of Wesker's plays are liable – *Chicken Soup* and *Chips* in particular. It is easy for writer, director and audience to miss that delicate balance of suggesting *potential* for change set against a convincing situation. It is Paul who states the complexity of the problem, at the end of his long monologue:

> I agree with you, Peter – maybe one morning we should wake up and find them all gone. But then I think: I should stop making pastries? The factory workers should stop making trains and cars? The miner should leave the coal where it is? (*Pause*) *You* give *me* the answer. (*II* 52)

Well, as they say, there ain't no answer to that – no quick and easy answer anyway, and Paul's statement is not only left unanswered by Peter's embarrassment, but is overshadowed by the spectacular but purely destructive ending.

The last word of *The Kitchen* is given not to Peter but to the restaurant owner, Marango. He has been making paranoid speeches at each appearance – 'I pay you well. Just work, that's all' (*I* 28) and 'Sabotage. It's sabotage you do to me' (*I* 61), so his insistence on his pound of flesh and nothing but his pound of flesh here rings horrifyingly and comically true:

32

Why does everybody sabotage me, Frank? I give work, I pay well, yes? They eat what they want, don't they? I don't know what more to give a man. He works, he eats, I give him money. This is life, isn't it? . . . What more do you want? What is there more, tell me? . . . What is there more? What *is* there more? (*II* 68–9)

As the stage direction hopefully remarks, 'We have seen that there must be something more,' and further elaboration is unnecessary. There has been an earlier attempt to bring in a positive value, the 'caring' of *Chicken Soup*, (when Peter, bleeding from his destructiveness, comments sarcastically of the Chef's outrage, 'Now he cares' (*II* 68)). But this is an isolated reminder, just as Paul's question is left dangling. In *Chicken Soup* Sarah Kahn, like Paul, recognizes the complexity of social reform – 'If the electrician who comes to mend my fuse blows it instead, so I should stop having electricity?' (*I* 73). But Wesker draws this recognition and her advocacy of caring into a complex final confrontation with her son's disillusionment. By comparison Marango's question is, as Wesker says, 'potent but simple', and effective though it is, it was necessary for Wesker to move on to the less pressurized and limited canvas of *Chicken Soup* to do justice to what had never been a simple view of society.

The film of *The Kitchen* was made during 1961 and was released while the play was still running at the Royal Court (and indeed the film company invoked a barring clause to veto a West End transfer on the grounds that it would compete with the film). The making of the film gave early hints of certain preoccupations in Wesker's career over the years to come. First, as Boleslaw Sulik explained in *Tribune*:

> The production, credits say, is by ACT Films, which means that it was set up and backed by the trade union of film technicians. Within our commercial system this is about the nearest we can get to a really co-operative venture.

And in particular, as opposed to the union's earlier, pot-boiling, job-creation projects this was 'the first real acknowledgement by the union of the potentially creative nature of their work'. This obviously foreshadows Wesker's future involvement in the trade-union-and-the-arts partnership envisaged in Centre Fortytwo. Secondly, along with the 'spirit of co-operation and purpose on the set' came 'the key part which Arnold Wesker was allowed to play throughout the production', similarly foreshadowing his increasing insistence on participation in stage productions – and which ironically led to quite the opposite of a spirit of co-operation in some cases.

Wesker had written *The Kitchen* as a stage play while a student at the London School of Film Technique, and Alan Brien was among those who commented on its cinematic aspects, a

> three-dimensional, Cinerama, working-day in the land of early Orwell. For once in the theatre the eye is free to track backwards and forwards in depth like the camera iris of a Gregg Toland or a Georges Périnal. The action is a series of striking tableaux superimposed on each other at intervals of a hundredth of a second. But each one stamps itself on the retina as an individual composition.

But curiously what sounds like ideal filmic material does not come over with this freedom and clarity in the film itself. As Wesker said, 'We were all deluded into thinking that because its action was fragmentary it was obviously film material' (TW p. 89). In the film the camera, but not the eye, has freedom to track where it will; the unit is the camera shot which makes choices for the audience, and while close-ups can concentrate on the individual better than the theatre can do, spotlights or no, they do therefore cut out our awareness of all those other cooks beavering away in the background. A couple of brief outdoor scenes are inserted (which Wesker later considered a mistake), but the more important difference is that the film uses real food – and with this takes a stride over the dividing line into total realism. The balletic, nightmare effect is lost, but the *New Daily* critic shrewdly pointed out that a new dimension had been added: 'implicit in the showing of large quantities of chickens and lobsters, as their limbs and flesh are hurriedly torn apart, is the thought that a day or so before they too have been living creatures' – merely another kind of kitchen fodder. (It was incidentally a school production, at Wandsworth and Mayfield Schools, which boldly decided both to have its food and mime it, by running a film of real food and 'mouths gorging in close-up' as a backdrop to the 'meticulous precision' of the miming.)

It is difficult to take the changes made for the film on their own merits, but the *Spectator* critic seemed to find the food and realism a successful alternative means of communicating Wesker's original intentions:

> I seem to have been about the only innocent at the press show who hadn't seen the play anyway and so I could look straight at it as a film and a very cinematic-looking treatment it looked to me. In fact it was the objects, the kitchen paraphernalia and the physical action (fish-slicing, onion-chopping, egg-beating, steam, rattle, the slither of greasy plates, the varied movements of things cooking at a ferocious rate, every kind of saucepan and frying pan, the over-powering sense of heat and panic speed: all intensely filmish experiences – you don't after all, get those eloquent close-ups of splitting sausages in the theatre) that struck just the right note of claustrophobia, hysteria, comradeliness.

The stress on objects and on physical action – including a fair amount of cooking – was in fact to be carried over into even the least naturalistic of the later plays (the strudel-making in *The Four Seasons*), but in this case Wesker concluded that these elements were not appropriate; that '*The Kitchen* is intrinsically a theatrical concept, and that to have made a film of it really required complete rethinking' (TW p. 89).

4

Chicken Soup With Barley

Chicken Soup With Barley, about the disintegration of a politically-conscious family, could have been written about the last days of that family; but no, I had to begin at the beginning, when the son was only a child of four, and take the play through twenty years ... And so you see this obsession with digging back as far as possible to beginnings, in order to explain the present. And all the time I'm worried in case a clue has been missed. (FF p. 113).

Wesker had started with the image of the last scene of the play, a powerful argument between mother and son, set in 1956, but, as he said, he decided to build towards it from an earlier stage in the family's life, so that as the play stands it opens with the warm optimistic togetherness of the East End, where the Jewish communist Kahn family – Harry and Sarah, their children Ada and Ronnie – and their friends, the whole community it seems, are uniting to block the Fascist Blackshirt march through their streets. But in the second act we have moved on to 1947, and Harry's shifty idealism has subsided into apathy, confirmed physically by his first paralytic stroke. Ada and her husband Dave, disillusioned by servicemen 'like animals' and office girls like 'lipsticked, giggling morons' (*I* 42), plan to drop out of industrial society altogether. Only Sarah and Ronnie are still committed and still optimistic, and though Ronnie is only a bookshop assistant he is going to be 'a socialist poet' (*I* 48).

In the third act, another ten years or so later, the rare visits from old friends mark the depression and isolation of the Kahns' 'last days'. Harry is almost totally paralysed and inarticulate, and Sarah is worn out. It is 1956 and the Hungarian uprising has been brutally crushed by the Russians. Ronnie returns from his cook's job in Paris to confront Sarah with his own loss of faith in communism. It is late, Sarah is tired, but she finally summons up strength to cry out that one *must* have faith in ideals, however much mankind fails in carrying them out:

Despair – die then! Will that be achievement? To die? (*Softly.*) You don't want to do that, Ronnie. So what if it all means nothing? When you know *that* you can start again. Please Ronnie, don't let me finish this life thinking I lived for nothing. We got through, didn't we? We got scars but we got through. You hear me, Ronnie? (*She clasps him and moans.*) You've got to care, you've got to care or you'll die ... You'll die, you'll die. (*He pauses at the door.*) Ronnie, if you don't care you'll die. (*I* 75–6)

It is a moving speech, but set against the apathy of the other characters, and addressed to the numbed and unresponding Ronnie, it is no clarion call to action – more of a voice crying in the wilderness. Even the assertiveness of the final sequence is less than totally positive. *The Kitchen* had ended with a question: *Chicken Soup* ends with the conditional '*If* you don't care ...'. It's only a little more optimistic.

Indeed the pessimism surrounding Sarah's 'care or die' speech puzzled many people during the first brief run of the play at the Belgrade Theatre Coventry and the Royal Court (1959). One critic, Patrick Gibbs, picked up Sarah's assertion that without the idea of brotherhood there can be no life: 'Since her own life appeared to be in shreds about her, I took this to be ironic, and the whole play to be a study in political disillusion'. Which to some extent it is, without the necessary implication that political disillusion is a good thing. Against Sarah's sustained line of principle the fallings-away of the other characters make a graph of downward curves. The once enthusiastic young comrade Monty Blatt becomes a middle-aged materialist – 'There's nothing more to life than a house, some friends, a family' (*I* 62) – as is foreshadowed in the decline of the weakest comrade of them all, Harry, who rushes to the comfort of home and mother while the others are struggling on the barricades. The title of the play is one of the few positive pointers to be found, even though the chicken soup in question does not figure on stage. It is mentioned by Sarah in an anecdote as given by a neighbour to Ada when she was ill with diphtheria and Harry had deserted his family. 'Ada still has that taste in her mouth – chicken soup with barley. She says it is a friendly taste – ask her. That saved her' (*I* 74). This human kindness, coupled with Sarah's own character and beliefs, are all that a would-be optimist could muster to support the view that Wesker writes propagandist plays with a cheerful hortatory message.

So one important function of the earlier, more hopeful scenes is to balance the growing depression towards the end. Suppose Wesker *had* gathered up his 'beginnings' into a present time-scheme, using the exposition, revelation and confession characteristic of Ibsen's technique. Ronnie returns from Paris to attack his dominant and loving mother with the failure of her ideals, just as does Oswald in Ibsen's *Ghosts*; Ronnie fears that he has acquired his father's moral lassitude – 'I've lost my faith and I've lost my ambition. Now I understand him perfectly' (*I* 72) – just as Oswald has inherited his father's venereal disease; and both young men were affected by their parents' imperfect marriages. Yet in the Ibsen play the effect is of the iron-hard pressure of past failures inexorably shaping the present. The Wesker play, however, allows some view of might-have-beens; and for the audience actually to encounter the youthful enthusiastic characters and their idealism dramatically establishes that idealism as a value worth fighting for.

What for instance would be lost if the only version we had of the past were filtered through Sarah's critical and Monty's sentimental reminiscences:

> MONTY: Everyone in the East End was going somewhere. It was a slum, there was misery, but we were going somewhere. The East End was a big mother. (*I* 62·3)

and

> SARAH: Ach! Horrible times! Horrible times – dirty, unclean, cheating!
> MONTY: But friendly.
> SARAH: Friendly, you call it? You think it was friendly to swindle people? (*I* 63)

Taken in the context of the last act, where friendliness has been lost without a great gain in physical well-being for Harry and Sarah, the result would be something more approaching the atmosphere of *Ghosts* or Wesker's own later play. *The Friends*: a unified, bitter regret, with a sense of waste dominating, but without the redemptive last scene of *The Friends*.

But as it stands, the first act of *Chicken Soup* successfully creates this sense of 'going somewhere': the movement, the rushing in and out, the fighting, the preparation of food, all vigorously express the purposefulness of the characters at this stage: 'Sarah Kahn characteristically picks up a red flag in one hand and a rolling pin in the other', as Irving Wardle put it. And of the 1978 revival, Sheridan Morley noted the 'upbeat *Fiddler on the Carpet* effect' and added that Wesker had taken care to qualify it from the beginning: 'in the midst of this first-act joy the father of the family is already nicking cash from his wife's handbags'. But the whole of this act with its sense of special crisis, urgent dialogue and manic activity is in a slightly different style from the subdued naturalism of the later scenes. The characters are a little larger than life, and perhaps there is an element of farce in the waving of flags and rolling-pins. As well as being useful as a deliberate foil to the later acts, this oversized activity is partly due to Wesker's basing it on his own childhood memories, amplified and gilded by later reminiscences. His reliance on material from his own experience has always been evident – 'yet another, I assume, in the series he has drawn from personal experience' J.C. Trewin was to remark of *Chips With Everything* not altogether approvingly – and from time to time it seems to lead to an interesting tension between Wesker's sense of the original 'real life', and its transformation into 'art' for the purposes of the play.

For instance, the Wesker family at the period shown at the beginning of *Chicken Soup* actually lived in an attic, and an attic set was originally specified for the first act. The eventual basement set was suggested by the director John Dexter:

> It was a Dexter idea which I thought was a good one, because you could see the feet of people running, so you had the opportunity to create a sense of crowds without having to employ more actors. And families did live in basements, it was only an accident that we lived in an attic and not a basement.

This then was an acceptable translation, as it did not contradict the essence of Wesker's memory: but reinterpretations of the characters were more problematic. The character of Sarah, based on Wesker's mother, has never quite been recreated the way he intended, and to him this truth to his original concept is more important than the effect within the play. In spite of Sarah's dominance in the play, her very positiveness can be unsympathetic; witness the stage direction which spells out her heavy-handedness in dealing with Harry's evasions: 'This is her well-meaning but maddening attempt to point out to a weak man his weakness' (*I* 14). To Wesker this is a two-edged quality:

> She could have been a patient, long-suffering woman who loved all the time and apologized for him and excused him, but she didn't, she fought him. Now this is a strength, but it is also a failing.

In the original production, Kenneth Tynan found Charmian Eyre's 'strident' Sarah 'rather too blatantly prole, commenting on the character rather than embodying it', a harshness underlined by Frank Finlay's more successful playing of Harry:

> Slumped, grinning, in his chair, Mr. Finlay mumbles his heart out so movingly that we are unable to distinguish between the petrifying of his body and the graying of his soul. This is a great performance.

And for Wesker too it was great because it reproduced exactly what he had envisaged and intended when writing the play. Finlay was able to respond to the text so 'accurately' as to mirror the character of Wesker's father:

> Particularly in one scene, where Harry screams at Ronnie, it came from such an area of truth that it sounded like my father, and in the performance at the Royal Court it so distressed my sister that she had to flee.

Sympathy for Harry may account for labels such as 'virago' that critics found for Sarah. In the text, Sarah seems the more sympathetic character, and it may be that one needs to *see* her nagging Harry, and more important to *see* the reactions of Harry and the children to what just look like eminently reasonable comments on the page. Apparently a better balance emerged in Tony Cornish's 1978 production, where the interaction of Sarah's strength and failing as a fighter came over. Robert Cushman described it:

> She emerges as a particularly fascinating type of the woman who loves humanity at the expense of those near her. Not that she neglects her family: her charity does not only begin at home, it is rooted there. It is very practical: at almost every moment of the play food is being cooked or eaten or a kettle brewed. But it is a charity fatally divorced from tolerance.

But he also used the words 'enthusiastic bullying' which suggests a tendency to the 'nagging shrew' type of interpretation that distressed Wesker's mother when she saw the play. Wesker intended the part to be played against the text: 'Apparently serious things were said by her with humour. Certain militant things were said by her softly. "You can't have brotherhood without love" – she would say something like that with a smile, she'd throw it away'.

Is Sarah's intolerance however as strongly written into the text as Harry's opposite failing, which is a tolerance fatally divorced from charity, in that his never doing anything includes his never doing anything for other people, even his own family? We see Harry stealing a ten-shilling note from Sarah's bag, and hear of his deserting his family while his daughter is dangerously ill – these weigh more heavily than Sarah's nagging, and at the same time justify it. Wesker's own wish is to see Sarah sympathetically presented, although 'it always upset me that the critics saw them [Sarah and Harry] in terms of one right and one wrong'. Yet it is not unfair to expect that the complaints and nagging that are in the text should be made to convey a certain amount of intolerance on the part of Sarah.

Related to this is the way her important last speech grows out of Sarah's character. There needs to be a hard edge to her character to support her position, and if too much is made of her motherliness – or of her 'credulity' and 'folly' as Robert Cushman saw it – then the validity of her final speeches will be undermined. 'The damage comes', Cushman went on, 'when Mr. Wesker, pulling himself together and remembering where he is, seems – as in Sarah's ringing curtain line "If you don't care, you'll die" – to put his full weight behind her.' The authorial weight *is* behind her at the end. 'Old Momma Courage', Francis King called her, and there is something of the problem here that Brecht had with the ending of *Mother Courage* – audiences *would* sentimentalize over Courage's brave persistence in self-destruction; and if the 'care or die' speech is just seen as an extension of Sarah's brave, simple mother-to-all-the-world personality, then it can be smiled over and dismissed.

So it is quite important to distinguish that Sarah's personality *in the play* can sustain the difficult position she is urging on Ronnie. Now, this scene was drawn closely from a similar confrontation between Wesker and his mother. When asked how accurate the final sequence was, he said 'I think I recreated the actual moment,

41

that more or less that's what she actually said. I can remember being marvellously moved and impressed at the way she rounded back at me,' but his view of Sarah is that she is as simple as his mother was – 'She was an innocent. She didn't understand at all the complexities of politics.' This corresponds to Monty Blatt's exegesis of Sarah's character:

> But she has one fault. For her the world is black and white. If you're not white so you must be black. She can't see shades in character – know what I mean? She can't see people in the round. (*I* 62)

Yet it is Monty who has swung from communism to political agnosticism because he is unable to cope with betrayals and disillusions. He has made a choice in black and white terms; Sarah here merely says 'And supposing it's true, Monty? So? What should we do, bring back the old days?' (*I* 61). Expanding on this is the last scene, she says:

> Now the people have forgotten. I sometimes think they're not worth fighting for, because they forget so easily ... You think it doesn't hurt me – the news about Hungary? You think I know what happened and what didn't happen? Do any of us know? Who do I know who to trust now – God, who are our friends now? ... If the electrician who comes to mend my fuse blows it instead, so I should stop having electricity? I should cut off my light? (*I* 73)

She says that she is a simple person, but she is perhaps not as simple as Monty. All her life she has fought both on the individual level and against the system, but it is not a blind instinctive struggle: as this speech shows, she is conscious of what she is doing, and aware of the alternatives. Her value of human beings is balanced by her disillusion with them; her confidence is qualified by mistrust; but she nonetheless makes the decision to go on fighting against all the doubts. She may be 'a simple person' but here she is making an existential choice that is rather more complex than that made by Monty or Ronnie.

This seems to be the point of revealing so many doubts and disillusions in the speech, only to contain and override them at the end. Admitting that the speech does show a complex and logical argument, Wesker still sees this as, for his mother, a temporary insight: 'Like many of the older communists, she was prepared at this point to pause and say, well, maybe, perhaps something went wrong. Nevertheless when that period passed, many of them forgot the doubts'. But *in the play* there is no passing on to a period of rationalization and hardening of attitudes; it retrospectively illuminates Sarah's life. And perhaps there is little real contradiction between Wesker's memories and their transformation into drama in this case, for it is not so much the details of political ideology that are at issue here, but a larger view of politics that extends to a philosophy of life, in which emotion ('Love comes now. You have to start with love. How can you talk about socialism otherwise? (*I* 30)) has a place it does not have in mere *realpolitik*. The 'caring' could apply to several other creeds as well as socialism. And Wesker qualified the 'simple' label:

> I can see you feel there is a contradiction in the play. Politically she is simple, emotionally she's not. She's a much more complex person emotionally: she had some very strong values. So if she's complex in the play, it's at an emotional level.

(The identity of Sarah and Wesker's mother confuses this statement: most of it refers to the former, the 'had some very strong values' to the latter.)

The argument about emotional complexity confirms that the Sarah of the earlier scenes should be both less shrewish than her critics saw her, and less good-natured than Wesker would have preferred: more real complexity in the first act would benefit the play, as a play, regardless of its truth to its origins, by supporting her awareness and penetration at the end.

43

5

Roots

Roots is not the illuminating and self-evident title that it might be: talking of an individual's 'roots' one is inclined to assume connotations of a rich family tradition and respect for the past. The play is concerned not only with these, but also, and sometimes contradictorily, with knowledge about the present time, understanding of the modern world, and the ordering of values by other criteria than mere tradition. Its message is a more social version of E. M. Forster's 'only connect', and a more accurate title for the play would offer an image of networks of interrelationships.

Admittedly, *Networks* is hardly a title to conjure with, whereas *Roots* suggests the organic development and wholeness of human personality which is as important here as it was in *The Kitchen*.

The connection with the other parts of the trilogy however is peripheral as regards plot, and in sharp contrast as regards subject matter. The heroine, Beatie Bryant, is engaged to Ronnie Kahn, who appears in the other two parts of the trilogy but remains unseen in *Roots*. Beatie is expecting him to join her on a holiday she is taking back in Norfolk, first with her married sister Jenny, then with her parents. Nothing much happens, except that we see Beatie's suppressed unease about the gap between Ronnie's intellectual, political and cultural interests, and her own limited horizons (and unwillingness to extend them). These qualities are shared by her family. Then, dramatically, as the whole family is assembled to meet Ronnie, a letter arrives from him instead, jilting Beatie. This shock provokes Beatie into a painful reassessment of herself and her assumptions, and into the very awareness and articulacy that Ronnie has despaired of her ever finding. Blackly ironic from Beatie's point of view, her breakthrough into being 'articulate at last' makes for an upbeat ending. Ronnie's determination to 'save someone from the fire', seemingly doomed by Beatie's stolid materialism, is suddenly seen to be justified. People can change for the better. Environmental influences can be counteracted. Beatie *can* grow roots.

Though this seems clear, the relevance of the title did cause some confusion to audiences. How could families so evidently stuck in the mud be called 'rootless'? Surely they must represent the roots that hold people back and drag them down. J. C. Trewin, defending Wesker against those who 'cannot believe that Mr. Wesker's earth-encrusted families exist', which they do 'in the villages where there is nothing to attract the tourist', nonetheless inferred that 'some of the roots we prize without considering them too closely need to be grubbed up at once'. And Alan Dent in the *News Chronicle* reversed both the meaning of the title and the message of the play:

> In the third act it begins to emerge that a young woman cannot really ever escape from her country roots, and that there is really nothing she can do about it unless she stays in town and stops interfering with her own rustic but contented relatives.

Another critic agreed with the 'unpopular (but surely undeniable) truth' that 'if these are our roots, the sooner we sever all connexion the better'.

This interpretation can only result from not *listening* to the play. Beatie's celebrated last-act speech spells it out: 'I am not talking about family roots' she says; and she is referring not only to herself – 'I come from a family of farm labourers, yet I ent got no roots' (*I* 145) – but to her rustic relatives as well:

> I'm tellin' you that the world's bin growing for two thousand years and we hevn't noticed it. I'm telling you that we don't know what we are or where we come from. I'm telling you something's cut us off from the beginning. I'm telling you we've got no roots. (*I* 146)

Even country people, in a rootless society, live superficially from hand-to mouth, materially and culturally, 'just like town people'. Roots here are what give a sense of belonging to a world that has purpose, instead of which her family are helpless passengers, ignored by those in power. Romantically, of course, a country community is traditionally supposed to retain a sense of the meaning of life, 'living in mystic bloody communion with Nature (indeed)' (*I* 147) as Beatie puts it. The Bryants' experience of country living is not only a complete contrast to what we have seen of the Kahns' East End life, which was articulate, lively, aware, even in its age and decline, but also to the situation in *I'm Talking About Jerusalem* where Dave and Ada import into the country all the ideals and romantic aspiration that the Bryants lack. The *Queen* critic's comment on *The Kitchen* – that there comes 'a point where manual labour is no longer dignified but, like a protracted illness, mortifying and degrading' – applies equally to *Roots*. Mr. Bryant cringes to the farm manager who plans to economize by sacking his assistant: 'I can manage, sir – 'course I can' (*I* 119). But he is later put on casual labour (at half pay) nonetheless. Mrs. Bryant, the stage directions explain, 'spends most of the day on her own, and consequently when she gets the chance to speak to anybody she says as much as she can as fast as she can' (*I* 106), but not to any great purpose: 'it's nearly always me listening to you telling who's dead' (*I* 114) grumbles Beatie, adding later 'Do you know I've heard that story a dozen times. A dozen times' (*I* 128). Mrs. Bryant's housework, 'cooped up in this house all day' and kept short of money, is as monotonous and dehumanizing as her husband's. Country surroundings make this no better:

> God in Heaven Mother, you live in the country but you got no – no— no majesty. You spend your time among green fields, you grow flowers and you breathe fresh air, and you got no majesty. You're mind's cluttered up with nothing and you shut out the world. What kind of a life did you give me?. (*I* 127)

As in *The Kitchen* then, the emphasis is on a way of life that has moulded Beatie Bryant and the other characters, and as with *The Kitchen* there were critical complaints about lack of incident. 'The stage takes reluctantly to the static depiction of uneventful lives' warned the *Observer*: 'The greater the play's success as truth, the less as good theatre'. This feeling bothered its first readers:

> George Devine was unhappy about it, and felt that I should combine the first and second acts into one act, and make the last act the second act, and write a new third act, in which Ronnie would appear. I thought this missed the whole point of the play, so it was not taken up by the Court. (TW pp. 81–2)

This would have resulted in a structure more like that of *Chicken Soup*, but inappropriate to the subject of *Roots*. It is necessary for the narrowness and limitations of Beatie's background to impress themselves upon us, otherwise her difficulty and her achievement in breaking away at the end are diminished. But the necessary display of monotony and bleakness is less camouflaged by back-chat than in *The Kitchen*: there the polyglot chefs failed really to communicate, but this was overlaid by the superficial give and take of gossip. In *Roots* the characters don't even chat much. The conversation of Jenny and her husband Jimmy Beales consists mostly of three and four word sentences, and there are long silences in which housework goes on without anything being said. The stage direction explains:

> This is a silence that needs organizing. Throughout the play there is no sign of intense living from any of the characters – Beatie's bursts are the exception. They continue in a routine rural manner. The day comes, one sleeps at night, there is always the winter, the spring, the autumn, and the summer – little amazes them. They talk in fits and starts mainly as a sort of gossip, and they talk quickly too, enacting as though for an audience what they say. Their sense of humour is keen and dry. They show no affection for each other – though this does not mean they would not be upset were one of them to die. The silences are important – as important as the way they speak, if we are to know them. (*I* 96)

And we *must* know them if we are to understand Beatie's predicament. So, the effect of the first two acts is a slow exposition of the routine of life in poverty-line households, where the bath has to be filled with a bucket. The original production, did not try to liven up or otherwise work against the leisurely development of the action, as T. C. Worsley acknowledged:

> John Dexter, the director, has been extremely daring in his use of slowness and silence. Accustomed to slickness and speed, we may find it difficult to accept his pace at first: but he insists from the start and soon has us with him. Ponderous slowness, pointless reiteration, stubborn taciturnity, cowlike vacuity – I have never seen these so perfectly caught on the stage. But the fact that they manage to be neither boring nor depressing is the highest tribute I can pay to Mr. Dexter and his admirable cast.

The cast performed, according to Kenneth Tynan, 'in a spirit of what might be called unromantic realism, though it is in fact – to revive an unfashionable word – nothing more or less than naturalism'. It now seems incredible that the 'unromantic realism' of talking with full mouths, the off-stage incontinence of the old neighbour Stan Mann, the 'bloodies' and 'buggers' in the dialogue were unacceptable, at least to provincial audiences, in the unpermissive early sixties.

The dialect itself was a stumbling block, not in being difficult to

47

understand, which it isn't, but in the expectations it sets up. Gerard Fay had pointed out in the *Manchester Guardian* 'that the regional play pure and simple is a scarce thing in the English theatre and that dialect, except in low comedy or one-act plays designed for drama festivals, is rarer still'. That this is a general rule, and that there is nothing specially non-serious about Norfolk dialect was confirmed by a comment on the adapted Lancashire dialect of a Rochdale production: 'The broad Lancashire speech has been so wedded on the stage to comedy that the divorce becomes difficult even in a play of ideas as this one is'. There is of course comedy in *Roots*, but the whole play could be undermined if audiences assumed that dialect meant they were to laugh *at* the characters instead of taking their predicament seriously.

But in practice it seemed to be pace rather than dialect that shifted the balance between comedy and 'play of ideas'. The *Times* and *Guardian* correspondents grasped this point firmly in David Scase's Manchester Library production, but on curiously opposite grounds: 'The pace set is that of brisk comedy and allows few opportunities for the creation of atmosphere or the expression of mood. Pauses, so far as possible, are avoided' said the *Times*; and 'He never makes the mistake of playing it as a simple rural comedy and he has captured the slow rhythm of country life where time is measured by the distant murmur of a country bus' said the *Guardian*. Perhaps they went on different nights? But the agreement that a fast pace highlights the comedy at the expense of understanding justifies both Wesker's original concept of two uneventful scenes, and John Dexter's restrained pace – Kenneth Tynan noted the avoidance of the comic pitfall in Dexter's production:

> And indeed, Mr. Wesker does want us to smile; but he makes sure that condescension in our smiling is replaced by compassion, and that we are always aware of the sad hard facts underlying the behaviour we find so hilarious. Taken separately, the details he accumulates are frequently comic; his achievement is to have set them in a context of such tangible reality that sympathy banishes belly-laughs. It is Chekhov's method, applied not to the country gentry but to the peasants at the gate.

In view of this stress on reality and the objections to overly realistic rustic language, it is interesting that Gareth Lloyd Evans, almost alone, had more qualified praise for the dialogue which 'runs between a faulty naturalism and an uneasy theatricality'. The naturalism of the Bryants' and Beales' casual conversation seems faultless enough: usually strain shows when deeper significance has to be reconciled with naturalism. The two characters in the play who have anything profound to say are Beatie herself, in the throes of her transformation, and Stan Mann, the one traditional countryman of the play, who sees some value in living and appreciating his surroundings. His expression of this balances well between meaning and the credible limitations of a country man's vocabulary and style.

> There ent much life in the young 'uns. Bunch o' weak-kneed ruffians. None on 'em like livin' look, none on 'em. You read in them ole papers what go on look, an' you wonder if they can see. You do! Wonder if they got eyes to look around them. Think they know where they live? 'Course they don't, they don't you know, not one. Blust! the winter go an' the spring come on after an' they don't see buds an' they don't smell no breeze an' they don't see gals, an' when they see gals they don't know whatta do wi' 'em. They don't! (*I* 107)

This is easy naturalism, with simple repetition and rhetorical questions for emphasis. The slow stop-and-start rhythm is totally convincing and quite unlike the more histrionic and voluble rhetoric of the Kahns and their friends. The control of different speech styles comes easily to Wesker, and he is deprecating about it:

> I always get annoyed with critics who talk about me being 'a master of dialogue'. Well, for Christ's sake, if you're not a master of that, what else? This is only a beginning, and shouldn't be the reason why a play is good, it's the least that one expects. (TW p. 89)

However, some of Beatie's speeches move away from this faithful realism and justify Wesker's remark that none of his plays are or can be simply slices of life. Her explanation of how she started her unlikely love affair with Ronnie is a continuous, subtly organized narrative, unlike her usual exclamatory style, and resembles Pip's similarly placed and similarly functioning speech in *Chips With Everything*:

> From the first day I went to work as waitress in the Dell Hotel and saw him working in the kitchen I fell in love – and I thought it was easy. I thought everything was easy. I chased him for three months with

compliments and presents until I finally give myself to him. He never said he love me nor I didn't care but once he had taken me he seemed to think he was responsible for me and I told him no different. I'd *make* him love me I thought. I didn't know much about him except he was different and used to write most of the time. And then he went back to London and I followed him there. I've never moved far from home but I did for him and he felt all the time he couldn't leave me and I didn't tell him no different ... (*I* 95)

There is nothing unnaturally complex about these sentences, but the refrain-like repetition of 'I told him no different ... and I didn't tell him no different' entwines Beatie's ironic secret viewpoint with her narrative; the very simplicity of her absolute 'I've never moved far from home before but I did for him ...' is touching – for a simple girl this is a great step. This speech dispenses for once with the 'blusts' and 'gals' which pepper the other speeches and lifts Beatie out of that specific formative background and into the realms of the universal and eternal.

We don't get this glimpse into what lies beneath the limited stoicism of the other characters, but, even in its uneasiness and misgivings, the speech is part of the preparation for Beatie's new vision in the last act. Some critics found her pentecostal break-through improbable, so it is relevant to notice how thoroughly the preparation is done. The change has been fermenting in Beatie for some time, as appears in her brisk demonstration of the pointless-ness (lack of roots) of Jimmy's territorial manoeuvres, her admit-ting to Jenny 'I couldn't have any other life now' (*I* 96), her dissatisfaction with her family's blinkered view of the world, and her willingness to talk constructively about her father's cut in wages. All these things are signs of her ability to understand Ronnie's teachings when examples are placed concretely before her: it is the power of generalizing outward from this that needs to be added. It is after all only too credible that a certain amount of selfish fear about her own disadvantages arising from her family's standards has sharpened her perception of those standards, now that she has others to measure them by.

And if anybody is going to break out of this rural defeatism, Beatie is the obvious candidate. Perhaps because she has been the spoilt youngest child, she is the liveliest and most outgoing of the family: as we have been told, 'Beatie's bursts are the exception' (*I* 92), and Mrs. Bryant says 'Thank God you come home sometimes gal – you do bring a little life with you anyway' (I 116). In the original production Joan Plowright as the first Beatie made the transition to articulacy universally acceptable. Bernard Levin reviewing the transfer to the West End, showered praise on every aspect of her performance:

> ... Miss Joan Plowright gives one of the greatest virtuoso performances to be seen on the London stage this year or for many years past. Pretty and touching, comic and absurd, warm and sure, before the end lost and hurt, at the last radiant in triumph, she dances her way (literally, at one point) through Mr. Wesker's marvellous prose and into our hearts.

And the *Jewish Chronicle* critic noted a detail of the final speech – 'Joan Plowright's chuckle as she cries "Why, it's me that's talking" gives a finishing touch to a performance that throughout has been delightful'. This acclaim led to the cautious proviso by Peter Roberts that 'I should not like to see *Roots* in an inferior production with an inferior cast'.

But as it happened *Roots* became the play that virtually every repertory company and amateur dramatic society in the country wanted to do. All over England reviewers waxed lyrical about provincial Beaties. It was not surprising perhaps that an actress as gifted as Eileen Atkins at the Theatre Royal Bristol seemed able to replace the irreplaceable Miss Plowright with 'vitality' and 'pathos', but most of the other leading ladies scored successes as well: at Rotherham the Beatie was 'a great personal triumph, a superb display'; at Reading the acting showed 'almost uncanny skill and sureness'; at Aldershot there was another 'superb performance', at Derby the actress was 'brilliantly acting her most demanding role' and at Birmingham Rep., (even in a production where the director David Buxton had 'taken the play gingerly between finger and thumb, tidied up the salty language, played down a lot of the forthrightness of some of the characters – and generally succeeded in making everyone far more self-conscious than they need have been') Rosemary Leach, 'for whom the part might have been written', gave a 'wonderfully alive realization of Beatie', another critic agreeing that she 'is without any doubt the definitive Beatie' and 'caps Joan Plowright's admirable performance'.

The play is virtually foolproof, as all these companies instinctively realized. Yet for Tony Cornish's 1979 revival, the National press was still thinking of *Roots* as Joan Plowright's play: 'The spirit of Joan Plowright stalked the stage last night, for it was she who turned this second play of Arnold Wesker's trilogy into a triumph all of 19 years ago' said *Evening News* critic Caren Meyer. So, predictably, there was slightly surprised praise from Michael Billington, for example, for Frances Viner's 'genuinely subtle' Beatie; in fact Irving Wardle in *The Times* surmised:

> that Frances Viner's performance, often extremely irritating and as mean as the surrounding family, is closer to Wesker's idea of the character. With Plowright you felt that she would be all right anyway; with Miss Viner it is a moment of real transformation when she breaks out of her inherited shell.

So in spite of surviving memories of Joan Plowright's creation of the role, nobody was able to claim that the play was even substantially altered without her.

In some ways *Roots*, because less historically focused than *Chicken Soup* but less timeless than *Jerusalem*, is more open to the charge of 'dating'. In the 1979 revival, however, twenty years after the first production, Michael Billington like most critics thought that Beatie's predicament and her struggles were as true as ever: 'Time has altered the play in one respect: the absent boyfriend Ronnie would today be preaching the virtues of pop, rather than high culture. Otherwise Wesker's play retains all its impassioned socialist humanity', though a minority agreed with Milton Shulman that 'Time, I'm afraid, has done a fair amount to undermine most of Wesker's optimistic premises. Increasing affluence has not encouraged farm labourers to appreciate Bach, buy tickets to the opera, read James Joyce or learn Spanish'. But is affluence considered so important in the play? Sister Susan's television was as far from giving her a window on the world as Mrs. Bryant's resolutely low-brow radio programmes. In *The Wedding Feast* (1977) the factory workers are of much the same social and economic group as the Bryants; their affluence is greater than the Bryants' was in 1959 and they have freezers as well as televisions, but only one woman character has made a breakthrough from this background to Marxist social consciousness – the remainder are merely better off in much the same commercial consumer society as enclosed the Bryants, proving Wesker's point that 'they will continue to live as before' (*I* 148). Beatie's conversion is so very persuasive that it overshadows the massive and intransigent nature of the social problem, to which her escape is the exception. Complacency about increased affluence (though this should not be overestimated as far as farm workers are concerned) is another red herring obscuring the real meaning of 'growing roots'.

6

I'm Talking About Jerusalem

With hindsight the *Jerusalem* play looks like a promising theme not quite securely realized in action. Ada, the daughter of Harry and Sarah Kahn, and her husband Dave Simmonds had already appeared in *Chicken Soup*, and both there and in *Roots* occasional mention was made of their removal to Norfolk so that Dave could make handcrafted furniture away from the industrial rat race. *Jerusalem* shows the course of this experiment, from moving in to moving out. In between, a series of successive disappointments – the apprentice leaves for more money in a factory, the idolized friend comes only to mock and criticize, the transport lorry carelessly ruins Dave's wares – makes the point of the play: that it is impossible to build Jerusalem in a sealed soap-bubble, and that for the would-be drop-out no man is an island, and hell is other people.

The uneasiness with which the play develops betrays that structurally it is pulling in two different directions. The *John O'London* critic said epigrammatically 'When Chekhov wrote the third play in Mr. Arnold Wesker's trilogy, *I'm Talking About Jerusalem*, he called it *The Cherry Orchard*,' and the first and last, moving-in and moving-out scenes do build up a Chekhovian web of allusions, misunderstanding, warmth and anguish from the texture of the Simmonds and Kahns interaction as a family. Yet this sense of an established way of life is not recreated in the middle scenes which are episodic and chronicle the comings and goings of characters who play their brief roles and depart. So as a Kahn family play *Jerusalem* lacks a centre, and as an episodic chronicle it is weighted down by a framework of family characterisation and atmosphere that is not essential to the Simmonds's experience.

Wesker himself was aware of a structural uncertainty:

I know that when I began Jerusalem, I wanted somehow for it to have a different feeling from the first two plays, that I wanted somehow not to have a conventional three-act play – somehow to break out. I suppose it must be considered the most flawed of the three, there's something wrong, and I think what's wrong is that there is this impulse to break

Patsy Byrne, Charles Kay and Joan Plowright
in *Roots*, Royal Court, 1959.

Chips With Everything, Cameri Theatre, Tel-Aviv, 1962.

out that I never quite fulfilled – until *Chips*, and in *Chips* it falls into place.

The Chekhovian label might seem contradicted by the reaction of several critics – that, as in *Roots*, a slow play was redeemed by what the *Yorkshire Post* reviewer called its 'blazing third act'. Milton Shulman said

> Suddenly, however, in the third act Wesker's undoubted talent blazes to tempestuous life and in Dave's denunciation of those who have laughed at his efforts, there is a compassionate urgency and vigour not often seen on the English stage. These moments save the play.

In fact these moments occur in the first scene of what is conventionally divided out as the third act, but really belongs with the series of encounters that take up the centre part of the play. In this scene aunts Cissie and Esther are staying at the Simmonds' cottage in its last-ditch metamorphosis as a 'guest house', and Esther challenges Dave to *talk* to them about his visions and problems. Her challenge turns into a justification of the industrialized, consumer-society comforts that she feels she's earned. But Dave for once explodes with 'I talked enough! You bloody Kahns you! You all talk. Sarah, Ronnie, all of you. I talked enough! I wanted to do something' (*I* 205), and defiantly he asserts 'you call me a prophet and laugh do you? Well, I'll tell you. I *am* a prophet' (*I* 206). For once his resentment of the uniformly negative attitude of the rest of the world (but is it totally unconnected with their decision 'not to bother to explain'?) boils over in excoriating speeches. But in the final scene, Dave is subdued, melancholy:

> Once I had – I don't know – a-a moment of vision, and I yelled at your Aunty Esther that I was a prophet. A prophet! Poor woman, I don't think she understood. All I meant was I was a sort of spokesman. That's all. But it passed. (*I* 215)

It is Ronnie who supplies the occasional feverish bursts of energy, wandering round helping to pack, singing ironic songs, making jokes. But he is more stricken at the Simmonds' failure than they are, and finally sinks to his knees 'in utter despair' (*I* 217). There are no blazing speeches to reassure him in this scene: the Simmonds communicate as usual, by what they *do* – 'they must indicate that they are going on' (*I* 217). Slowly their example stiffens his defi-

55

ance, until he rises and shouts at the indifferent evening sky 'We
– must – be – bloody – mad – to – cry!' (I 218).

Ronnie is a difficult role, in that he has to balance self-consciousness and sincerity, too imperfect to be a mouthpiece, but too
humanly concerned to be merely the light relief. Richard Findlater
felt that the writing was right, but the performance didn't come
off at the Royal Court.

> For me the prime failure is in the performance of Ronnie, presented
> here as a kind of madcap, balletic Puck, full of merry quips and wry
> quotations, prancing lithely about the stage from one pose to another
> and listening intently to himself as he does his sophisticated best to play
> the holy fool. Ronnie strikes attitudes but like a person, not like an
> actor.

This is important, in spite of Ronnie's small role in the play,
because, according to A. Alvarez, Wesker allows Ronnie 'to steal
the limelight and confuse the artistic issues with his almost irrelevant intensities' so that 'in *Jerusalem* when Dave and Ada are
facing the bitterness of their failure to live Socialism, we are
suddenly told that the real tragedy is that their disillusion has
smashed Ronnie's hopes'. Alvarez sees this as an autobiographical
blind spot in Wesker:

> Ronnie, in fact, is Wesker's second weakness. He is taken in by the
> image he has created of himself. So Ronnie is allowed to make continual
> demands of people and give them in return only gush, charm, glibness
> and self-pity. In *Jerusalem* he emerges finally and frankly as a prig, and
> a prig, what's more, about life, forever mooning and maundering while
> the others clear up the mess and put the fires out after them.

But was this a blind spot in the author, or a feature of 'David
Saire's hollow, gushing performance'? In the text, Ronnie's flights
are mostly cut brutally short, usually by Dave – Ronnie's first line
in the play is one of advice 'Gently now ...' to those actually
working, but is followed by Dave's retort 'Instead of standing
there and giving orders why don't you give a bloody hand?' (I 155).
And to Ronnie's last, perhaps 'glib' protests, 'too hastily' trotted
out, Dave counters bluntly 'I know your kind, you go around the
world crooning about brotherhood and yet you can't even see a
sordid love affair through to the end' (I 216). Dave's criticisms
show that the gush and self-pity are recognized as such by the
writer, and Wesker later contended that what Ronnie actually *says*

indicates honest uncertainty and several characteristically contradictory traits, and that Ronnie had never been played to his
satisfaction.

Wesker did play the role himself once, on tour in Rome, where
Gwen Nelson thought that his acting corrected his writing – the
part was overwritten, but he underplayed it, and it worked. It is
not so much that Dave is there to cut Ronnie down to size, but
that Ronnie exists to show the wordy theorizing that Dave and
Ada reject. Acts are to speak louder than words. And yet ... and
yet ... They turn out to be wrong about words when, in one of the
most moving scenes, Ada returns from the hospital padded cell
where her father Harry is dying, and tells how he at first failed to
recognize her, then accused her of hating him:

> it's not true, it's never been true ... But perhaps I didn't tell him I loved
> him. Useless bloody things words are. Ronnie and his bridges! 'Words
> are bridges' he wrote, 'to get from one place to another'. Wait till he's
> older and learns about silences – they span worlds. (*I* 194)

But she herself insists on words in the Genesis I-spy game she plays
with her child; and Aunt Esther says sadly after Dave's furious
reply to her criticisms 'You want to build Jerusalem? Build it! Only
maybe we wanted to share it with you' (*I* 207). Words are the main
way of sharing things for the Kahns.

The Genesis I-spy episode is another of those overtly didactic
passages, like Beatie's exposition of the 'L'Arlésienne Suite' in
Roots and the Cutty Wren ballad in *Chips*, which read as embarrassing and self-conscious, but make a surprising impact in
performance. Here, although Alvarez thought it 'terrible', Kenneth
Tynan singled it out as one of the passages that was 'lovingly
observed and lambently acted'; Bernard Levin felt that it redeemed
excessive political didacticism and was 'of such beautiful and
shiningly poetic a quality that it lifts the faults of the play bodily
on to an entirely new level'.

The acting overall was not as impressive as in the earlier two
plays. What Richard Findlater called 'the inadequacy of the cast'
was detailed by Mervyn Jones:

> Wrong accents, wrong clothes (a country squire in white gloves), wrong
> moves (this character refuses to sit down and immediately sits down)
> go far beyond the permissible quota. The key speeches are delivered
> without feeling or understanding.

And John Dexter's direction did not win as much approval this time: the pace, 'alternating between extreme rapidity and exasperatingly over-sustained pauses, gave the text little chance to breathe', wrote *The Times* critic, while Alan Pryce-Jones in the *Observer* blamed the actors for not coping with 'the pouncing emphases, swift darts of emotion between laughter and tears, and perilous revelations of feeling'. Mervyn Jones detected an over-anxiety to avoid the accusations of slowness that *Roots* had attracted:

> One very marked characteristic in Wesker's plays is that the characters are always doing something – working, cooking, eating, singing, dancing, carrying things about. This gives the picture, or rather the sculpture, of their lives, a certain dense and deep reality; the talk which bursts from them as they move is a part of their lives. But in this play it is decidedly overdone, and they would be more credible if they would only sit still for a minute.

And he turned a critical eye on Jessie Robins' virtuoso performance as Aunt Esther, which had been praised by everyone else: 'When a production is such a hit-or-miss affair, all balance can be upset and the meaning sadly obscured by a vivid, aggressive performance of a minor part', and a 'piece of ruinously good comic acting came from Jessie Robins'. This, he thought, 'put a spotlight on a fault in Wesker's craftmanship: a lack of decision as to which are the essential scenes and the essential characters'.

This points back to the undecided structure of the play, hovering between naturalistic development and episodic accumulation – indeed, there had been two more little scenes in the middle in the original production at the Belgrade Coventry, which were excised for the London transfer.

Many were disappointed that *Jerusalem* did not knit together the whole trilogy. (Some critics had wistfully looked out for Beatie Bryant in *The Kitchen* – first staged after *Roots* and before *Jerusalem* – so no doubt her re-entry for a honeymoon ending had been confidently awaited here.) In theory there is the opportunity to reconcile the political awareness of *Chicken Soup* with the unregenerate rusticity of *Roots*. *Jerusalem* does qualify the optimism of *Roots*: saving one person from the fire is nothing to feel complacent about if even the dedicated Dave and Ada can't 'live socialism' in the teeth of customers and bank managers. The 'hindsight' mentioned at the beginning of this discussion is relevant because the play inside *Jerusalem* that is struggling to get out is, as their associated titles suggest, *Their Very Own and Golden City*. The survival of Dave and Ada, living to fight another day, is more encouraging but less forceful than the fate of the *Golden City* characters, who become corrupted and disillusioned as well as defeated; and there are more dimensions to the message of the later play because of its pronounced psychological element, which interacts subtly with its social theme. Social experiment is the central concern of both plays, but where *Jerusalem* is still trying to relate this concern to the Kahn family's position, *Golden City* has moved towards the psychologically analytic phase of Wesker's next few plays.

Chips With Everything

> Those who have put Mr. Wesker into the category of the dreary four-walled realists must now think again. He has broken right out of the naturalism of his Trilogy and has found a form that allows him to express his feelings and ideas implicitly without any of that preaching which was the weakness of the earlier plays.

This was a splendid development as far as the *Financial Times* critic was concerned, but it doesn't need much imagination to foresee that 'lack of realism' would be the objection raised by those who did not like the movement towards stylisation. The artifical rules and regulations of the situation of the play, defined by the eight-week training period of a group of new National Servicemen in the Air Force, in themselves place the action in a comparatively arbitrary world; more so than in the restaurant kitchen or any normal workplace. The actual routine – the drill – of this self-contained world is more of a spectacular image *for*, rather than an example of, the dehumanizing monotonous routines that the average person has to carry out in the real world. And the image is heightened because drill is so divorced from immediate usefulness, as opposed to *The Kitchen*'s chopping, frying and boiling.

On the other hand the story of the main characters against the air force background takes on more significance than Peter the cook's slow simmer to the boil in *The Kitchen*. Pip Thompson, a banker's son, is working out his Oedipus complex by refusing to join the air force hierarchy as an officer trainee. He is, like Peter, a rebel rather than a revolutionary, though he starts well by pushing his mates into recognizing their own unnecessary deference and the officers' patronage, without sentimentality or inverted snobbery. The title of the play comes from his scathing summary: 'Chips with every damn thing. You breed babies and you eat chips with everything' (*III* 17) Yet this is the root of Pip's failure as a revolutionary, for if he does not love or even value anything in his fellow conscripts, why is he troubling to raise their consciousness against the officers? The officers, who feel that his rightful place is with them, want to know this too; the suave Pilot Officer, dismissing comradeship and social conscience as possible motives, homes in on power – Pip wants to control, organize, direct. He is – apparently unconsciously at first – using the other conscripts in a personal power struggle against the establishment.

The contradiction in Pip is quite clear in his behaviour even early in the play: in the first act he organizes a silent, fast-moving and very funny raid on the coke heaps to supply the hut stove. It involves a kind of relay race with chairs, buckets and stools to get the raider back and forth over the wire netting in between a sentry's regular appearances. It is very complicated and it is planned and directed by Pip alone, so that afterwards the others are full of admiration for his initiative. 'You always need leaders' (*III* 46) agrees Corporal Hill, and though Pip protests that 'Each time you say "always" the world takes two steps back and stops bothering' (*III* 47), his own actions have said the opposite. Then at the end of the play, when the hut scapegoat, Smiler, helplessly returns from trying to run away, the others silently, without discussion, without a leader, *without* waiting for Pip to organize them, unanimously unite in defying the officers, defending Smiler against due punishment. Pip finds it impossible to be just one of the lads, and he siezes the only way of reasserting himself: he smoothly excuses and defuses this potential mutiny, at the same time putting on the uniform of an officer trainee – changing sides, in short. The hutmates are not arrested, Pip has become an officer, and Smiler is kept back for more weeks of (punitive) 'training'.

Philip Hope-Wallace was not sure that this climactic betrayal really came across in performance:

> though the play in its human warmth of humour and the intense sincerity of its compassion did succeed a second time in bouncing me into accepting it and going all the way with it emotionally (if not rationally) I still believe that there is a very large hole in the second half, an ellipsis which leaves us (or nine out of ten of us in the audience) a little confused as to what has finally *happened*.

And there were certain references to Pip as a 'middle-class messiah' that implied that Pip was being taken as a straightforward reformer. The convolution of his motives – admitted father-hatred, contempt for his comrades' docility while using it, self-consciousness – makes him a far more flawed and even twisted character than any of those Wesker had shown so far, and marks the break-through into new psychological territory.

Given the complexity of Pip's character it may be that the structuring of the climax complicates rather than illuminates 'what has finally happened' in the murky recesses of Pip's mind. His change of sides is diffuse in that it comes in two stages – first, he is demoralized when he recognizes his own power motives, and second, he realizes he is incapable of becoming one of the chip-eating mass. And because Wesker is reserving Pip's overt change of allegiance for the final climax, his state of mind between these two stages – during which he rejects his friend Chas's appeal for help, but won't say why – is not explained to us. On the other hand the fact that there had been a betrayal, and that it was of profound emotional consequence, impressed most of the audience powerfully: for Pip and Smiler, in different ways, it marked 'the imminent death of two souls', said Harold Hobson.

Altogether *Chips* had a far more emotional impact on stage than the text would suggest – as Hope-Wallace had noticed; and several scenes were mentioned as being particularly effective in this way: 'I dare you not to be moved by the scene between Chas and Pip in the first act', said the *Sheffield Telegraph*. This is the dialogue in which Chas, fascinated by Pip and antagonized by his deliberately provocative tone of superiority, gradually begins to communicate with him:

> PIP: Mm. I'm not sure why we started this,
> CHAS: Well, you said we got enemies, and I was saying –
> PIP: Oh, yes.
> CHAS: There now, you've lost interest. Just as we were getting into conversation you go all bored. (*III* 40)

Both are ready to take offence and to misunderstand, but a moment of comradeship ensues when both admit to being only sons and having lied about having several brothers, spoilt almost imme-diately by Pip's using the wrong tone in replying 'I suppose so' to Chas's 'Can I come?', and Chas has almost to shout down Pip's misinterpretation of his next remark about education:

> CHAS: Let me bloody finish what I was going to say, will you! You don't listen. You don't bloody listen.
> PIP: I'm sorry –

CHAS: Yes, I know.
PIP: I'm listening.
CHAS: Oh, go to hell – you –
PIP: I'm sorry, I take it back, don't shout, I'm listening.
CHAS: I didn't say *I* thought it'd be easier if I was more educated – I said *you'd* think it'd be easier, I thought *you'd* think it. And I was just going to say I disagreed – then you jumped. (*III* 41)

The suspicion, the raw susceptibility, the effort to overcome these and bridge the gulf, are painful and touching at once, and the scene ends with an interesting sequence during which Pip and Chas simultaneously expound their two separate trains of thought – respectively, on inverted snobbery about manual labour, and about the superficiality of university-acquired polish. This does not mean that they are 'not listening' again. They are communicating by matching monologues, and these monologues are parallel, making the same point in different areas – which is what Pip's and Chas's relationship should be like. This takes place in act one scene eight, and the corresponding scene in act two – that is, scene nine – contains Pip's refusal to respond to Chas's plea 'I could grow with you' (*III* 62). Either the capacity to relate to one of the chips-with-everything class on a personal level was never there, or it has been destroyed in the demolition of Pip's revolutionary image.

Their dual monologue is one of several alternative styles of dialogue, another of which is naturalistic conversation – already familiar from the trilogy – as between Charles and Pip above, or between the crowd of conscripts in the hut. Early in the play, with minimal preparation and no apology, comes Pip's well-organized long speech, reminiscent of Paul's in *The Kitchen* or Beatie's in *Roots*. Pip replies obliquely to the taunt 'You don't mind being a snob do you?' by beginning formally 'One day, when I was driving . . .' (*III* 16), and he goes on to describe the strange *depaysment* or sense of alienation he feels in the 'cheap cafe', among the people and surroundings of a level of society that is totally alien to him.

Nothing, of course, in the cafe is particularly extraordinary; Pip's sense of shock comes through his hypnotic focus on little details:

photographs of boxers, autographed, and they were curling at the edges from the heat . . . a rag that left dark streaks behind which dried up into weird patterns . . . grains of dirt in the lines of his face' (*III* 16–17).

Like Beatie's speech, this one has a recurrent refrain: 'I don't know why I should have been surprised' (*III* 16–17). Knowing about a different culture intellectually is by no means the same as realizing that difference fully, with all the senses. That is why Pip makes this speech at this point: it is tangential to his subversive programme, but plants a seed of doubt about his position: with these feelings of alienation, what kind of relationship is he going to develop with the 'side' he has chosen in the class war?

Pip is almost speaking to himself here, and Smiler's speech, which comprises the whole of act two scene ten during which he is 'running' along a road, and represents the passing of several hours, is more incoherent, more of a disjointed interior monologue.

> I'LL GET AWAY FROM YOU, YOU APES! They think they own you – Oh my back. I don't give tuppence what you say, you don't mean anything to me, your bloody orders not your stripes, not your jankers nor your wars. Stick your jankers on the wall, stuff yourselves, go away and stuff yourselves, stuff your rotten stupid selves – Ohh – Ohhh. Look at the sky, look at the moon, Jesus look at that moon and the frost in the air. I'll wait. I'll get a lift in a second or two, it's quiet now, their noise is gone. (*III* 63–4)

The changes of topic and feeling here have to be held together by the rhythm of running, a problem for the actor. John Dexter remembered

> Ron Lacey in agony with Smiler's running away, Arnold and I seemed powerless to help him find the balance between the reality of the situation and the formal rhythm of the words, a problem he only finally solved for himself 24 hours before the first night. (P & P December 1962)

On the other hand the more public, 'set piece' speeches have a rhetorical rhythm that would be hard to miss, as in Corporal Hill's designedly uninterruptable drill instructions:

> You nit, you nit, you creepy-crawly nit. Don't you hear, don't you listen, can't you follow simple orders, CAN'T YOU? Shut up! Don't answer back! A young man like you, first thing in the morning, don't be rude, don't be rude. No one's being rude to you'. (*III* 20)

And the officers likewise in ritual fashion trot out their own particular rhythms of meaningless bureaucracy – 'Discipline is necessary if we are to train you to the maximum of efficiency, discipline and obedience' (*III* 22) – or obsessive logic – 'and your huts must be spick and span without a trace of dust, because dust carries germs, and germs are unclean' (*III* 23).

The public speeches are all to some extent rituals, as are the bayonet practice, the tormenting of Smiler and so on. This is where the formality, the artificiality of the military setting supports Wesker's use of stylized language – except that the resulting stylization of the officer class was not acceptable to some of the audience. The *Times Educational Supplement*, disliking the whole play, saw the officers as 'simply grotesque caricatures as far removed as possible from any sort of reality', a view which Clancy Sigal in *The Queen* modified somewhat:

> For one thing, Wesker does not really know very much, as indicated in his previous plays, about the upper class as people; he must rely therefore on caricature. In a basically non-naturalistic play such as *Chips* this is not a fatal misapprehension. Class domination is a more subtle proposition than Wesker lets on in most of his scenes, although it is obvious, principally from Pip's lines, that Wesker fully understands this.

Wesker himself categorically denies being vague about the officer class:

> Well, it has been said that the reason why those characters seem to be more stereotyped is because I haven't experience of them. I don't agree. I deliberately said to myself, I am not going to make them rounded characters out of any sort of liberal impulse. However rounded I might make them, they still stood for what they did. (TW p. 90)

In the late sixties when several dramatists were experimenting with 'comic-strip' stylization (for instance Charles Wood in *Dingo*), the caricatures, being so obviously intentional, tended to be judged successful on their own terms. Wesker however didn't see himself as anticipating that trend: 'And even so, the way they spoke and the way they behaved is not caricatured, it is very real.' (TW p. 90)

Another dramatic peak in the action which seemed to convince most critics, even against their will, is the Naafi Christmas party, the scene of Pip's first manipulation of his mates into confrontation with the officers. Instead of the expected 'dirty recitation' and pop song they offer the creepily chilling old ballad the Lyke-wake Dirge, and the traditional revolt song, The Cutty Wren. Mervyn Jones wasn't making any allowances for a 'basically non-naturalistic play'; for him the scene was 'totally out of place in realistic theatre':

> 'The Cutty Wren' is a medieval folksong with a covertly rebellious meaning. The song is familiar to a coterie of middle-class intellectuals. The link between folksong and the working-class in industrial Britain, whether we like it or not, was long ago broken; or rather, the folksongs of our time are cast in the idiom of jazz and its derivatives. Yet Pip is shown successfully halting a pop number to make way for 'The Cutty Wren'.
>
> The scene, the high point of John Dexter's admirable direction, is impressive as an isolated theatrical effect. But as soon as one reflects on the possibility of it actually happening, one has to admit that it is the most sublimely silly scene put on any stage for quite a while.

The theatrical effect captured most people, however – 'a moment of theatre-magic of the rarest kind', the *John O'London* critic called it, 'a moment that catches the breath', and the otherwise unfavourable *Times Literary Supplement* review conceded that 'the famous Naafi revolt, for example, which means nothing as read and by any logical or realistic consideration provokes the gravest doubts, comes over as a powerfully theatrical symbol of an ideal dear to Mr. Wesker's heart', underlining Wesker's perennial and usually ignored contention that 'my plays *do* work in the theatre'. And Arnold Kettle makes a similar point in the context of discussing non-naturalistic techniques: 'The singing of "The Cutty Wren" ... comes off triumphantly, though I doubt whether Wesker is seriously suggesting that any actual RAF station party was every quite like that'. Kenneth Tynan gave the fullest description of just what theatrical effect was made of the bare six verses given in the text:

> The accompaniment ... begins with a spoon rapped on a bottle and swells until every man on stage is stamping and clapping and singing. It is an electrifying and entirely credible moment: folk art becomes, before one's eyes, a contemporary possibility.

The tendency of reviewers to consider theatrical effect as the province of the director (or actors) led some critics to credit John

Dexter with all that was successful in the play. J. C. Trewin voiced the customary caution: 'I think we ought to ask how it is likely to appear without a production of this uncommon quality and without a regimental sergeant-major to oversee the training'. In this case the question could in fact very briskly be answered – were it not for the London critics' habit, as also with *Roots*, of ignoring the rest of the country – because Wesker had allowed almost simultaneous premieres in London, Sheffield and Glasgow. As a gesture against metropolitan navel-gazing, he had offered the play to eight provincial companies to open at the same time. Only Glasgow accepted, and Sheffield, not one of the original eight, volunteered. It is interesting that the local Sheffield reviewers echoed London's general praise, whereas the Scottish critics disliked the play almost unanimously. Irving Wardle saw both London and Sheffield productions, and of the latter he observed:

> The result has nothing like the polish of John Dexter's production at the Court, but in some ways I suspect it is closer to the anatomy of the original ... What comes over is a bitterly personal expression of loathing for the class tyranny of Service life; and it is this which is muffled in the naturalistic Court production.

This is a telling point, for it seems that Geoffrey Ost at Sheffield was the most successful of the three directors in coping with the vexed caricature aspect of the officers – which might be because he was not as anchored in naturalism. In an article in *Plays and Players* he explained how one of the trickier problems had been overcome, as the actors playing the officers had

> appeared at rehearsal to drop naturally into a stylized method of acting, which might have been at odds with the more naturalistic approach of the other characters. It was however realized that there was no need to reconcile them at all; in fact, it seemed finally that this effect could be enhanced on occasions by lighting as was done in the Pilot Officer's final scene with Pip when looming shadows of Established Authority towered over the cowering, beaten conscript. (P & P July 1962)

Callum Mill at Glasgow had, as he said in an accompanying article, been seeking a compromise: 'A playwright who is so obvious in his intentions but juxtaposes hard realism and an almost poetic and stylized quality is difficult to get in focus. Finding a style that was consistent for the play was not simple and here and there I may not have done Wesker full justice ...' (P & P July 1962). His reviewers saw through the changes of gear, interpreted them as weakness rather than strength, and, like Peter Hamilton, thought that 'the writer has been betrayed into working as a cartoonist'.

In London Dexter was aiming in the play as a whole, at a certain stylization *through* naturalism:

> First must come accuracy in the reproduction of detail, the accumulation of details to grow into a nightmare of discipline which drives out individuality. Only when these physical problems are solved can the play break out and the audience accept that maybe it is not just about life in the RAF. To me all problems in the theatre are technical problems, but if technical problems can be solved, emotional problems cease to exist. (P & P April 1962)

Not only the nightmare of discipline, but the dreamlike way the characters are carried swiftly, almost helplessly, along by the military organization depends on smooth direction. For instance, the change from act one scene two to scene three goes as follows:

> HILL: That's fast, that's fast, into the hut and move that fast. Into the hut, into the hut, in, in, into the hut. (*Looks at watch. Pause.*) Out! I'll give you ...

And in this pause, the night has passed, the boys have trotted off stage then back on, and the Naafi set has to disappear and be replaced by the parade ground. At the Royal Court, John Dexter had cramped conditions to work with, but at least he had five weeks of rehearsals: at Sheffield and Glasgow the directors had equally limited resources and only a fortnight to organize them. As Geoffrey Ost said, there were twenty-one scenes and 'the aim was to achieve a method in which the "picture" dissolved and broke up at the end of each scene and came together at the beginning of the next without jerk or effort', the main problem being that a lot of these scenes involved the hut interior and nine army beds. Two revolves were considered and rejected, the eventual solution being to leave some beds permanently upstage, with downstage beds on two trucks that could pivot them away and substitute backings that became the outside of the hut. At Glasgow Callum Mill had the additional difficulty of a steeply raked stage:

some pieces were flown in, but the problematic beds were moved by the characters – 'the conscripts themselves, as in real life, acted as scene-shifters, moving the beds through the walls of the set'.

Glasgow, however, had some compensation in a Corporal Hill (Michael O'Halloran) who had actually spent his early days as an instructor in the Scots Guards, and this possibly helped give the drill scenes a snap and dash lacking at Sheffield. Dexter had the famous RSM Brittain instructing his actors, and used a military approach himself in rehearsals:

> Hard angular moves, rhythmic rather than emotional delivery of lines, an insistence on instant response without question, to all direction, produced an atmosphere loaded with resentment, but not unlike that of the early stage of primary training and from which we progressed to being able to turn discipline on and off as we needed it. (P & P December 1962)

The hostility has to be there, the master-servant (even slave) relationship between officers and men, so that the moments of confrontation can flash into dangerous life. The meaning of the pattern into which the recruits have been fitted during the course of the play is displayed in the final scene, the coda to the action, in which the men march on for their Passout Parade, guided by Corporal Hill '... together in time. I want you to move as one man, as one ship, as one solid gliding ship. Proud! Proud!' (*III* 68). Flags are flying, music is playing (and, what shook the audience in 1962, God Save the Queen was being played just *before* the end of the play, not just after, so instead of standing up for it as usual they were caught disrespectfully sitting down) and as the previous scene of Pip's betrayal has shown, the unity achieved so confidently here is a defeat for both individuality and for any unity valuable to the men themselves.

There were many objections to the allegorical level of the play, in its claim to be showing the operation of class distinction and class warfare – naked and unashamed in the RAF hierarchy, without the blurring and softening of society at large. Clancy Sigal as an American was less disturbed by the play's moral (though he also thought Wesker's previous plays had been handicapped because 'so many of his strongest characters were socialists or communists'):

As a dramatic diagnosis of the disease of class, *Chips With Everything* marks evidence of steady growth, of a persistent hammering at the heart of the nation from a different, more delicate, angle than formerly.

Wesker was, he said, a 'moral thermometer for the rest of us'. Harold Hobson was ambivalent about both disease and diagnosis:

> As a member of the Athenaeum and MCC I view it with misgiving; as a dramatic critic, I will cheer till I am hoarse and black in the face. This is the Left-wing drama's first real breakthrough, the first anti-Establishment play of which the Establishment has cause to be afraid.

But how afraid need the Establishment be of any play? Robert Muller:

> All the values that are cherished by most of those who will pay for their stalls are here brutally assaulted. What will the West End public reaction be as they are shown the inexorable process of degradation that transforms a bunch of raw recruits into efficient war robots ... no doubt, to quote the author, they will listen but they will not hear. They will tolerate and ignore. They will applaud but they will not act.

Perhaps it was some feeling like this that made Wesker at this point decide that like Dave in *Jerusalem* he had talked enough; now he wanted to *do* something. In 1963 he formally renounced writing plays for the time being to devote himself to setting up the Centre Fortytwo project, but he recollects quite soon feeling the need to avoid 'literary constipation' and beginning to write *Their Very Own and Golden City*.

8

Their Very Own and Golden City

Now, people always need to know that someone was around who
acted. Defeat doesn't matter; in the long run all defeat is temporary. It
doesn't matter about present generations but future ones always want
to look back and know that someone was around acting on principle.
(II 147)

Early in *Their Very Own and Golden City* (1966) this is what Jake
Latham, an old local Labour Party leader says to the hero of the
play, Andrew Cobham. Andrew at first takes this to heart; he
doesn't go the way of Peter the cook, destroying blindly and
helplessly, or of Pip – changing horses mid-stream. He is altogether
more effectual than his predecessors, yet he too fails in the end,
and his failure like Pip's contains overtones of betrayal. *Golden
City* belongs at the end of the first phase of Wesker's writing, in
which he kept returning to the theme of the failed rebel/revolu-
tionary. *The Four Seasons*, produced earlier than *Golden City*,
really belongs to Wesker's next, more introspective phase, and was
in any case actually begun after *Golden City*. Curiously, while
echoing the plot line of *I'm Talking about Jerusalem*, in that both
show bold experiments being defeated by financial, personal and·
social problems, *Golden City* also obviously reflects Wesker's own
more recent experience with the hopeful rise and eventual crumbling away of Centre Fortytwo, as *Jerusalem* had foreshadowed it
– his life imitating his art, then transformed once more into art.
Wesker, however, like Dave, admitted defeat rather than compromise and betray his ideal, as Andrew does.

Andy Cobham is an apprentice draughtsman, who in 1926, with
his friends Stoney and Paul and his sweetheart Jessie, has a youthful vision of building new golden cities all over England, indeed,
of creating a whole new society. Later becoming an architect of
exceptional talent, married to Jessie but now prompted by Kate
who loves him, he sets out to put the vision into practice – six
golden cities, paid for and owned, houses, shops, factories and all,
by the subscribers who will live there. The obstacles to the vision
are of the same kind that afflicted Dave and Ada – and Centre

Fortytwo: money, opposition of authority, scepticism, ill-will and again money. Crucially, although the houses are built, the trade unions refuse to finance the essential industry – which means employment for the inhabitants. Through years of holding meetings, gaining planning permission and appealing regularly for the unobtainable industrial investment, Andy grows more callous and ruthless, and eventually compromises first by abandoning an already subscribed five cities to save the sixth, then by allowing private enterprise to supply and own the city's industry. So instead of a social experiment, a template for change in society, Andrew is left with a rather better designed New Town, a knighthood, and self-disgust.

Many reviewers noted at once the correspondences between the Golden Cities project and Centre Fortytwo, right down to the parallel of the six cities and the six festivals that Fortytwo had put on. Originally the play had been conceived as 'an epic drama on the rise and fall of a trade union leader' – epic in the Brechtian episodic sense. But compared with the equally episodic but spectacular, blackly humorous *Chips*, it met with a cool reception, and some blamed this on the basic experience that Wesker was using. This was 'no job for a playwright and no theme for a play either', said Barry Norman, and Wesker should 'hand over Centre Fortytwo to someone else and write a *real* play again'. David Nathan lamented the 'prolonged and humourless enthusiasm' of the protagonist; W A Darlington had the impression that the characters 'spend most of the evening haranguing each other on committees – a form of dialogue to which I have to force myself to listen'; and Philip Hope-Wallace 'simply found that this immensely sincere statement quite failed to speak to my old sentimentalist's heart'.

Evidently it was feeling – of which the plot apparently has plenty, from enthusiasm to anguish – that was lacking. Mary Holland suspected that 'this play should have sent us out of the theatre as passionately moved as we were by *Roots* or *The Kitchen*', and blamed the director William Gaskill:

Where the production most unforgivably fails is in a lack of humanity. More than most playwrights Wesker is dependent on well-balanced direction. Play him for warmth and his work degenerates into a sloppy mush of sentimentality, play him for intellectual content and his ideas are shown up as all too human emotions.

Dexter, she thought, had previously brought the two extremes together by 'showing the ills of society through the wrongs which people inflict on one another', whereas Gaskill had played down emotion.

> The play teems with characters who demand our understanding. The hero himself, his wife trapped in her ignorance but begging to be valued as something more than a child-bearer, the aristocrat's daughter with her cold socialism and unhappy intellectual sneer, the old trade-unionist. All of these are alienated into symbols mouthing speeches, and to distance them further still they are usually frozen into awkward poses at the end of a set piece.

If the play 'demands a humanity and lack of self-consciousness in the playing to match that of the writing', the writing itself is not blameless, she went on, with its over-long political speeches and clumsy construction, though again the 'production in a series of darkly lit episodes does not help'. Others noted the frozen poses and general darkness: J. W. Lambert wished 'that Christopher Morley's ingenious sets were not so uniformly glum and that William Gaskill's direction did not quite so often freeze the characters to mark the end of scenes (of which there are thirty-odd) – thus imparting a reverential air to proceedings already amply earnest'.

It seems clear from the text however that the effect should *not* be austere. The play opens in Durham Cathedral where the young friends are inspired by a sense of incredible beauty: 'Magic. Discovery' (*II* 135), as the stage direction puts it. The second half of the play is meant to have 'a sense of purpose, bustle, activity and – most important – growth and decay' (*II* 180) and eventually 'visually, for the first time we must see and feel the magic and excitement of a city growing' – hopefully with the 'magnificent abstract set of a building site' (*II* 198). In the revised text several of the scene changes have their rapidity spelled out and indeed blend into each other to pre-empt directorial freezes, and when Wesker directed the play himself in Denmark he felt that the faster pace and the 'brilliant set of Hayden Griffin' made the play work. Certain other unobtrusive but influential revisions he made to the structure were all on the side of increasing the positive impact in performance. Originally Andrew's life unfolds in separate scenes up to the first public Golden City meeting, with flashbacks to the young friends in the cathedral, planning and dreaming. After this, the Golden City project proceeds as a 'continuous scene' and a 'flash-forward' – that is, a projection, a hypothesis of how Andy's life will develop up to 1990. Its hypothetical nature was not insistent, however, and in the revised version Wesker makes the whole of Andrew's adult life a 'flash-forward', the 'present' being his hopeful youth in the cathedral, which stays on stage throughout, with Andy and his friends as it were imagining the depressing prospect of the future. Looking back to the original production, Wesker refers to 'the mistaken and crippling decision (with which I foolishly agreed) to have one set of actors play both the old and young protagonists' (*II* 127). Apart from being more convincing, two sets of actors are a reminder of the distinction between the original idea, and what *might* be made of it. As long as the young characters assert their presence and vitality, the choices of the older characters need not seem inevitable. And without extra scenes of dialogue the revised version has the young characters appearing in the second-act continuous scene (which originally they did not), taking over lines from their 'elders': '*Two scenes now happen together*', a revised stage direction says, '*the present interleaves with the future. A Cathedral scene becomes a counterpoint to a Monday Meeting scene*' (*II* 187). And where the older Andy loses Paul's and Stoney's friendship by dropping the other cities they have been supervising, simultaneously we see the young characters 'wander off, wrapped in their own discussions' (*II* 193) still hopeful, still friends. By the end of the play Andy has aged so much that, as Wesker's note says 'if one set of actors plays both parts, then old Andrew will have to be left on the stage after the bridge scene since it will be impossible for him to change back' (*II* 205) – the final scene being a Cathedral scene for the young friends – and so 'Old Andy must deliver Young Andy's lines wearily in contrast with the gaiety of the others, to retain the sad irony' (*II* 205). In this last scene, the friends have lingered too long and been locked into the cathedral for the night; they panic, but 'Paul's found an open door ... We knew the door was open ... Because we're on the side of the angels, lass ... and people are good' (*II* 205).

This of course offers fairly explicit hope that other and better ways of building Golden Cities remain possible. Wesker's original motive was based on the position that instinctively, as an artist, my inclination is not to indulge in morbidity and pessimism, and so I flinch from the oppressive ending. And this is in direct conflict with experience, which is so often oppressive and depressing. And the form of the flash-forward gave me the opportunity to cheat, to have two endings, in fact: the ending of the young ones, which is optimistic, and the ending of the reality-stream. The problem is, whether the weight of the reality-stream isn't more depressing than the weight of the innocence-stream is encouraging. (TW p. 93)

In revising the play, he decided that the balance *was* more depressing than otherwise, and thus made these alterations which in the end make the innocence-stream *into* the reality-stream, leaving Andy's adulthood as a 'dark dream'.

If set and pace can be made to reinforce the optimistic visionary element in the play, how much of the actual dialogue is 'austere'? Andy's efficient demolition of his old friend Jake in public debate is both savage and significant – D. A. N. Jones deduced that 'the result must be (as in the real-life Bevin–Lansbury duel, so closely copied) that the rank-and-file support Cobham but dislike him, love Lathan and vote him down. This is a subtle and touching kind of battle'. Other confrontations, between Andy and the local planning chairman, have a surprising snap in them, but it is true that the formal speeches do bulk large – to the TUC, to the Monday Meetings, and so on. The speeches themselves are well made, varying as in *Chips* from young Andy's storytelling –

> Now they only want the boat to carry them for a little way, for a short time, but as they build it they sink holds and erect decks, they build cabins and kitchens, they give it a polish and lots of sails and all they do is travel a hundred miles from one piece of land to another. But that's daft, isn't it? (*II* 178)

– to the older Andy's practised rhetoric, with repetition, alliteration and all:

> Old age laments, leave lamentations till the grave – *we* know! *We* know what holds men in a movement through all time – their visions. Visions, visions, visions! (*II* 179)

But the official, role-playing speeches at ministry, cocktail parties and committees outweigh the more relaxed scenes between friends, even despite further injection of youthful innocence and gaiety.

The character of Kate particularly suffers from the effect of her calculated and assertive speeches. Whereas Andy clowns his equal assertiveness, there is little exaggeration evident in Kate's lines, though Wesker, who was concerned that there should be more sympathy for her, wrote in some new stage directions – '*She offers him a lovely smile*' (II 151) and '*She sits. Utterly spent. Almost near tears*' (II 193) – to soften the effect of her pushiness. Still, as Andy says, 'It's the tone of your voice, it gets in the way ... I'd agree with you if only your voice didn't sneer at your words' (II 150–1), and her absolutes – 'I want ... you must ... it's my nature to' – accumulate against her.

Wesker had conceded that 'Of course it's too ambitious, the theme belongs to the cinema, it stretches across more time and action than the theatre can properly handle' (II 127): D. A. N. Jones, agreeing that the play 'packed in too much', had suggested Wesker should 'scrub the women'. Yet this would amputate a possibly undeveloped but nevertheless essential limb. What Wesker was saying in *Fears of Fragmentation* is the moral of Andrew Cobham's career: Andy's increasing compartmentalization of his life – his detaching himself from Jessie his wife, his withdrawal of real concern from his private practice – is both harmful and delusory, because the ability to compromise and cut corners spreads to his ideals and the Golden Cities too. The first hint of callousness comes with his insensitive overkill in defeating Jake in the debate: 'Was it fair to say I "hawked" my conscience all around?' asks Jake. 'Be careful of your cities, that's what I'm saying' (II 165). And his relationships with the women show Andy's personal deterioration. One of the most moving speeches in the play is given to Jessie when she protests 'I'm not a fool; I've been made to feel it often enough, but I'm not a fool ... there's a wrong somewhere'. She goes on:

> Don't you know what I'm saying? Don't you hear what I'm telling? I don't mind being inferior but I can't bear being made to feel inferior. I know I'm only a housekeeper but I can't bear being treated like one. Wasn't it you wanted to treat everyone like an aristocrat? Well, what about me? I don't claim it as a wife, forget I'm your wife, but a human being. I claim it as a human being. (*Pause.*) Claim? I'm too old to stake claims, aren't I? Like wanting to be beautiful, or enthusiastic, or in love with yourself. (II 197)

Even the assertive Kate has ended up living her life vicariously through Andy, tied to him and unfulfilled, a social situation Wesker underlines with a revised stage direction – '*Maitland, since women are only appendages, ignores Kate, who moves away to listen from a scathing but dignified distance*' (II 186) – and which Andy accepts. If anything the women's role could well be extended, and some of the scenes set in the 'corridors of power' cut out, to achieve not concentration but the delicate balance between public and private lives at which Wesker was aiming.

9

The Four Seasons

The critical reception of Wesker's next play, *The Four Seasons*, was so hostile that Wesker was amazed – 'The critics went berserk!' (TW p. 94) – but added that 'Even for the most intelligent and sane critic, it still is a shock to go expecting one kind of play and to receive another'. Different it certainly was. Earlier Wesker had announced that it was to be 'a love story about two people', and in spite of the mockery of some columnists – 'Oh, one of *those* love stories! How square can you get?' – this is exactly what it was. In four episodes corresponding to the four seasons, the protagonists Adam and Beatrice appear in a deserted house; in winter Adam tries to thaw her speechless misery, in spring they fall in love, in summer quarrels reminiscent of old quarrels begin, and in autumn they part – all this without any explanation, background or other influences.

These obvious differences from his earlier plays prompted several people to an assessment of Wesker's new position. The *Jewish Chronicle*, thinking of *The Kitchen*, pointed out 'He has dabbled in the abstract before'. Others thought the play manifested features that were new but unsuccessful, while applauding the experiment for its own sake. Philip Hope-Wallace dismissed the piece as 'pretentious and utterly ineffective as a piece of drama' but added 'I respect Mr. Wesker for the sincerity and for having the courage to try it at all': encouragement echoed by the *Times* critic – 'One admirable hall-mark of the younger dramatists is their willingness to go on experimenting with new forms'. But again, he didn't like the results of the retreat from naturalism:

> Though Mr. Wesker is constantly alert to the explosive undertow present in any intimate relationship, perceptiveness does not of itself constitute drama. The flaw in his play is that he totally excludes the outside world. He does not admit that a love affair is no less subject to economic and social pressures than anything else.

In a long and sensitive review Mervyn Jones also offered

> a salute to his courage ... because the trend of contemporary criticism

is to mark out each writer's proper territory and rebuke him if he dares to break out of it . . . the play is at its best when attention is concentrated on the man and the woman, on what is happening within and between them. The external aids in terms of activity – painting walls and making cakes – are a weakening concession. With these devices, Wesker does what he knows he can do easily and what does not belong in this play.

Jones wondered whether the 'vacuum' impression worried people because it had not been carried out thoroughly enough; the initial abstraction was undermined by the isolated mention of shops and lectures – 'Either we don't need this framework, or we need more of it'.

Abstraction was the message of the set in this production, though in a later adaptation for television, Wesker based the set naturalistically on his own Welsh cottage. Zbynek Kolar, whose work Wesker had admired before asking him to design the set, built two flats as walls, with other furniture sliding on and off from the wings, and an abstract overhead design of 'balls and aerials' as the Scotsman critic described it. 'A handsome if slightly shopwindowfied stage picture' thought Ronald Bryden, and Philip Hope-Wallace also placed the set in the 'faintly Bond Street shop window class'. Penelope Gilliatt, hostile to the play, was not won over by the beauty of the design: 'At the head of Zbynek Kolar's set there is a beautiful abstract complex of telephone wires, but I never saw a place less connected to any world', and for her the very beauty, significance and isolation of objects on stage drained them of robust existence – 'Beatrice puts symbolic white paint on the walls, makes symbolic gold *lamé* curtains and a matching skirt, and buys a symbolic napkin ring ("We're building a home")'.

But how else is one to stress the eternal and universal? For the message of the play is more absolute than in Wesker's earlier plays, and as Martin Esslin observed, 'Once we have cottoned on to the symbolism of the four seasons, once we know that they will follow their inevitable, relentless course (and we catch on after a maximum of three minutes!), the play is doomed to run on its tramlines to the bitter end. There will be, guaranteed, no surprises'. Why should this lead to 'the boredom of predictability' however? After all, 'inevitable' and 'relentless' are terms of high praise in a tragedy – but then *The Four Seasons* is not a tragedy, not even a love tragedy. Wesker is not offering a world-picture in which Fate, or the gods, or God, or any other great absolute is in conflict with Man. *The Four Seasons* is offering a psychological determinism: 'We never recover, never' repeat the characters. One false step predetermines the next, precedents are renewed, and, as Esslin says, tramlines laid down. Adam initially betrayed a childhood sweetheart at school camp, and this boyish incident is presented as having biassed his adult life and established a pattern that wrecks his marriage and subsequent love affairs.

In one of the few references to Beckett, Derek Malcolm in the *Guardian* said 'Beckett and others have said all this and more a great deal better'; in theory one can rebut much of the sweeping condemnation of two-handers, cyclical forms and abstract settings by pointing to, say, *Happy Days*. In theory: but comparisons with Beckett were probably so thin on the ground because *on stage* the play is very evidently *un*Beckettian. Wesker did not intend the names 'Adam' and 'Beatrice' to be taken as meaning 'Man' and 'the Beloved' (indeed, a French production changed the names to Alan and Catherine and avoided charges of excessive 'symbolism'), and these two lovers are not, in their specific behaviour, *all* lovers.

This is the only one of Wesker's plays so far to press the message of inevitability. In the most pessimistic of the other plays there is somewhere a hint of what could be done, or what could have been done, to alter events, or to begin afresh with better success. The lovers are in fact indulging in something Wesker elsewhere condemns – the justifying of a personal failure by pretending it is a universal law (Macey in *The Friends* recognizes and avoids it; Boomy in *The Old Ones* does not).

Therefore, whatever the treatment of dialogue and detail of action, there would be this weakness of unjustified inevitability at the centre of the play. But the dialogue grated on many, though there is an interesting difference *in kind* between what seems to have worked, and what was singled out for criticism. In all his plays Wesker shows skill with different speech forms, particularly in rhythm – the rapid, running, inclusive sentence of the Kahns, the short remarks of the Bryants – rather than in vocabulary or imagery. So here, the prose rhythm stressed by repeated words or particular constructions was built into speeches that were noted as impressive. Here is part of Beatrice's monologue spoken beside Adam's sick bed:

Peace, majesty and great courage – never. I've found none of these things. Such bitter disappointment. Bitter. Bitter, bitter, bitter. And out of such bitterness cruelty grows. You cannot understand the cruelty that grows. And I meant none of it, not one cruel word of it. And he knew and I knew and we both knew that we knew, yet the cruelty went on. (*II* 102)

The repetitions are not only rhythmic or attention-catching devices, nor just pleasant assonances, but key words for analysing the all too understandable retaliatory games-playing. It reads well, and was praised, for instance, by B. A. Young, but, like others, what he didn't like was the 'tired old imagery'. It was phrases like 'I have a golden eagle for a lover' and 'my skin breathes' that were cited as objectionable over and over again. Wesker

> wanted to create a heightened and lyrical language. Of course pretentiousness had to be avoided, but the problem of using current English dialogue lay in its impoverishment; it is a real and disturbing problem (*II* 118).

but the audience's associations resisted Wesker's choice of phrases. Dusty Wesker advised her husband to cut out 'autumn soft skin' as it sounded like a soap advertisement, and though it is now deleted from the text, it stayed in for some performances and two critics pounced on it with the same objection. It may be regrettable but response to language is an intractable thing – better to invent a new dialect, as Arden did in *Armstrong's Last Goodnight*, than keep striking the wrong associations, the wrong tone. 'To seek the depth by altering the language is fruitless' Mervyn Jones summed up, because 'Language, to carry conviction, must have an idiom common to the author and his audience'.

Curiously the *Times Educational Supplement* whose reviewers had consistently disliked Wesker's early plays, found *The Four Seasons* far superior to these, and blamed any faults in the dialogue on the English language itself, in an odd apologia:

> If he happened to be French and writing in French, perhaps the text would be tighter and more tactful. But he is not to be blamed for failing to be French, nor the play for failing to be a translation from the French, in which case it would have been judiciously praised.

It was Martin Esslin, in his usual precise and analytical fashion, who listed and defined the various effects that left other critics feeling affronted. He agreed with Mervyn Jones about the half-heartedness of the play's abstract style, though his preferred solution was different: like others, he noted the change from Wesker's early naturalism, but he drew a parallel with early twentieth-century German drama, which like Wesker's work reacted against naturalism in two different directions, expressionism and neo-romanticism – though not, like Wesker, all in the same play. Thus, Esslin concludes, Wesker has combined expressionist characters with neo-romantic atmosphere-through-language, and 'burdened his play with an inner contradiction which is bound to lead to disaster', a contradiction in which the play 'strives to create atmosphere and therefore cries out for solid detail – and gets nothing but a surfeit of visual and verbal symbols'.

The major solid detail of the play was mentioned by everyone *except* Esslin, and that was the episode in which Adam makes a large and spectacular apple strudel, watched rather grudgingly by Beatrice. The strudel-making is very real, and therefore on a different level from the stage conventions Wesker was using to avoid naturalistic representation – Beatrice's supposed winter-long immobility, for instance. 'The process of making apple strudel is a very dramatic one and involves patience and experience. But actors learn to fence – who not to cook?' (*II* 121) says Wesker's note to the play, and Julian Holland commended the way Alan Bates as Adam 'correctly drew out the pastry to its proper transparency by using the *back* of his hands in the approved Austrian manner'. Its very reality pulled it away from the fabric of the rest of the play. Penelope Gilliatt quoted Stanislavsky's discovery that 'one of the most fascinating things that can be done on stage is to fry an egg', and maybe such cookery has the sure-fire upstaging effect of performing children and dogs, but, the *Sheffield Telegraph* said, 'When the most absorbing part of a play is an actor's onstage production of an elaborate apple strudel, something somewhere is wrong with the work as a whole'.

10

The Friends

Six friends – all between the ages of thirty-five and thirty-eight –
gather in one house, in one room, ignoring the bankruptcy of the
chain of interior design shops they have set up, because one of the
six, Esther, is dying of leukaemia. And after Esther's death, half-
way through the play, the friends, watched by the older, paternal
store-manager, Macey, go to pieces, not just because of the loss of
their dominating mother-figure, but because self-doubt, dissatisfaction with the past, disillusion with the future, fear of aging,
have undermined their own hold on life. 'Tired of living and scared
of dying' as the song says, they are crumbling with self-pity.

Not a comedy, then; Esther herself cries: 'It's depression time
again' (*III* 93). And not a play that sounds much akin to *Roots* –
yet in a reversed image *Roots* is the play it most resembles. As in
Roots, there is a stubborn resistance to be overcome; as in *Roots*,
a final upbeat scene forces a new vision on the unwilling characters,
though the mood of *The Friends* is the reverse of Beatie's determined cheerfulness, and the single figure who breaks through into
understanding at the end, Simone, is able to drag the other friends
with her. Wesker said: '*The Friends* can be seen, on analysis, to
have many of the same preoccupations as *Roots*' (TQ 28 p. 6), and
there are even verbal echoes such as 'no – no majesty' (*I* 127; *III* 80)
and 'the apple doesn't fall far from the tree, does it?' (*I* 145; *III* 123).
As Wesker keeps repeating, all he is concerned with is making
some order out of the chaos of experience, and characters like
Beatie – who says 'No wonder I don't know anything ... God in
heaven Mother, you live in the country but you got no – no – no
majesty ... Your mind's cluttered up with nothing and you shut
out the world' (*I* 127) – enact the same quest for order, as does the
far more sophisticated Manfred, Esther's brother:

> Our trouble, Crispin, us lot, the once-upon-a-time bright lads from up
> north, is that we've no scholarship. Bits and pieces of information, a
> charming earthiness, intelligence and cheek, but no scholarship ...
> Do you know, new knowledge disrupts me. Because there's no solid

rock of learning in this thin undernourished brain of mine, so each fresh discovery of a fact or an idea doesn't replace, it undermines the last; it's got no measurement by which to judge itself, no perspective by which to judge its truth or its worth; it can take no proper place in that lovely long view of history scalloped out by bloody scholarship, because each new concern renders the last one unimportant. No bloody scholarship, us. (*III* 83)

This is the main theme of the play – the problem of dealing with disorientation, the sense of having no system of values. Manfred there is looking hopefully to 'scholarship' to provide the ready-made solutions: Macey mocks him for buying 'whole libraries, from professors who die, desperately hoping their books will give him their cleverness' (*III* 91). Similarly Roland, Esther's lover, who at one time had wanted to be 'a voluptuary' is seen contemplating 'the sound of velvet' and 'the tiniest shifting of everything in the room': he is 'turning into an aesthete' (*III* 79); and Macey mocks him in turn: 'an aesthete? It's possible? He's had an operation or something?' (*III* 88). Then he slashes his back with a razor, to share (and somehow alleviate? He hasn't thought it through) Esther's pain; a little later he burns pound notes one by one. These are flailing gestures, founded on no coherent beliefs; as Simone says 'You won't come to terms with death that way' (*III* 111). Tessa, in spite of Esther's belief that 'women are natural revolutionaries' (*III* 106) – that is, constructive – is a destructive person. 'What's left worth the while to do?' (*III* 117) she asks; it is she who smashes her guitar and throws over the beautiful eighteenth-century chair, and she, like Manfred, longs to be young again. Crispin, usually bad-tempered, hides his habit of sleeping with old women for money, but his guilt over this is not supported by any moral, ethical or other basis for judging it right or wrong.

These four are thrashing about wildly for some means of justifying their lives, as Esther's death forces the retrospect upon them. Esther herself is the most positive member of the group: the paradox is that, though dying, she is the only one who really wants to live, in the fullest sense. As the play opens, she is giving 'Long lists of all the things I care about and why. Who do I hate, who do I love; what do I value, what do I despise' (*III* 78) – *she* knows the answers. Because she wants to live, she is like the one just man in the Bible whose existence could justify and save a whole city; she herself is a witness to the value of going on living, 'what's worth the while to do'.

Simone, the sixth friend, is the outsider and scapegoat because she alone comes from a more privileged middle-class background, and it is she who fights back against rejection and the confusion of her friends. Yes, she asserts, some things *are* more worthwhile than others, for dependable reasons. To counteract Manfred's defence that they lack the spirit, the sheer energy to re-found their lives at this late date, she brings forward the body of Esther: raising the body she moves it as if Esther were sending signs to them:

> A strange scene begins; at first it seems hysterical, then macabre, but finally must become the natural actions of people trying to find their own way of both showing their love for the dead and trying to overcome their fear of death, or at least trying to come to terms with the knowledge of death. (*III* 125)

And, because they must not think that Esther's death made her love of life invalid, Simone repeats, as she waves the dead woman's hand 'She wanted to *live* ... *She* wanted to live ... She did! She wanted to live' (*III* 126). This 'resurrection' image was given to Wesker by a Romanian director, who described a Romanian village custom:

> When someone dies, they lay the body on a catafalque and the mourners line up against the wall while the elders of the village dance, with phallic symbols – sticks and things – in their hands. And the dance becomes frankly erotic, even obscene. They whip themselves into a frenzy until finally they get the actual body, take it under the armpits, and dance with it. So there it is, this dead body, being danced with. It's some sort of release, the mourners laugh, and begin to dance themselves. This struck me very powerfully as a manifestation of the desperate need that men have to survive the knowledge of death: they will create extra-ordinary rituals for themselves so that they can live more easily with it. The image stayed with me when I was getting ready to write *The Friends*. And became the final image. (TQ 28 p. 8)

The resurrection of Esther is not savage or frenzied, let alone erotic or obscene; it is transformed by the tenderness of the friends into a moment of relaxation and acceptance. A difficult scene to play: J. W. Lambert saw it as 'what amounts to a surprise ending' but for Jack Sutherland the scene was among 'the most embarrassing I've watched in a theatre'.

However, for nine-tenths of the play, the desperate confusion of the unregenerate friends holds the stage, and Charles Landstone remarked rather dubiously that 'it is a tragedy that so many finely expressed ideas should have been allowed to tumble over each other without forming a coherent whole', and, citing Wesker's programme note (taken from his own unpublished *New Play*) about being confused by too many passionate beliefs, Landstone concluded: 'If the ability to transmit this passion on to the stage while preserving the confusion is to be regarded as an achievement, then he has brilliantly succeeded'. The *characters*' confusion is meant to be there, as the subject of the play: but the final double 'solution' – the existence of values, and the lifelong necessity of working these out – is not cut and dried, is not terribly specific, and does not come across with the force of Beatie Bryant's last speech. The problem is more complex than Beatie's, because more psychologically confused, so a single breakthrough is hardly to be expected; in addition, the final sequence with Esther's body is a stage metaphor for hope and persistence which did not convince many critics, and so, whether the fault lay with the writing or the production, the ending was less forceful than the stage metaphor that ended *Chips*.

A more successful visual metaphor was supplied by the set; in spite of occasional objections ('the headquarters of the metropolitan tat trade' said Iain Hamilton in the *TES*) most metropolitan critics appreciated the huge cluttered sombre bedroom. Rosemary Say, otherwise disappointed with the play, liked 'Nicolas Georgiadis's set, solid and graceful within the awkward space provided by the Roundhouse stage. Against a background of outsize foliage he has set dark sloping panels that bring exactly the right feeling of claustrophobia into the sick woman's bedroom'; J. W. Lambert lists in more detail the 'art-nouveau writhings in coarse brass, a more than lifesize brass peacock, a gleaming steel DNA model. Against the back wall an immense bed; over it hangs a poster portrait of Lenin. It is a set that needs to be seen in colour, for it is the shades of colour, rather than the bald outline, that build up the well-lived-in atmosphere.

'*The Friends* is quiet chamber music', John Barber wrote. And Wesker himself had said, bravely, 'I wanted to write it like a symphony' (TQ 2 p. 78). Perhaps a septet can never quite achieve symphonic volume, but counterpoint and harmony are evident in

the writing. The opening has not Wesker's favourite two strands
of monologue but three:

> ESTHER: Except the sound of French, that's beautiful; and Russian
> icons and pre-Raphaelites and Venetian chandeliers.
> ROLAND: Last night I slept very soundly. Long and deep.
> MANFRED (*reading*): 'The electron is a completely universal funda-
> mental particle ...'
> ROLAND: I can't remember the last time I slept so soundly.
> MANFRED: 'It is stable and long-lived. For all practical purposes it is
> indestructible and is at present in the universe in inexhaustible
> numbers ...'
> ESTHER: And Baroque churches and houses, fountains and market-
> places and the music of organs and Norman arches and wine and the
> cooking of friends and the sound of friends. (*III* 76)

And an even more difficult counterpoint brings the first act to a
close, just before Roland discovers that Esther is dead: Crispin is
trying to comfort the two women, while Manfred simultaneously
explains how his contempt for the working class has undermined
his youthful enthusiasm.

> CRISPIN: Peace –
> MANFRED: Waste!
> CRISPIN: – and silence.
> MANFRED: That's what I really wanted to say.
> CRISPIN: Blessed peace and silence.
> MANFRED: We're too old to pretend. (*III* 109)

Elsewhere D. A. N. Jones noted the

> cross-currents of conversation when the diffident, lady-like voice of
> Lynn Farleigh (as Simone) talking of order and justice, is punctuated by
> the brusque, workmanlike rebukes of Anna Cropper, as Tessa. By this
> antiphonal device, together with the recapitulation to key words and
> images, the intelligent, verbal argument is brought some way towards
> the condition of music.

And at the other extreme, the long uninterrupted set-piece speeches
that Wesker likes are fairly distributed among the friends, as
distress, drink and tiredness relax their inhibitions. Esther's final
speech, setting out the dialectic of rebels and revolutionaries,
twentieth-century novelty and twenty centuries of accumulated
human endeavour, was impressive: Charles Landstone described
Susan Engel as Esther as 'magnificent in her final death speech'.

And Ian Holm as Manfred had the longest speech in the form of one of Wesker's educational set-pieces, a resumé of his recent scientific reading, delivered as a mock-lecture on the discoveries of physicists from 1897 to 1930. A note to the text says 'It is of paramount importance that the actor makes as much sense of this précis as possible while at the same time clowning the story' (*III* 101). Again, the unrelieved two pages of solid text look totally undigestible and undramatic, but in practice came off as a *tour de force* by Ian Holm.

Wesker's subsequent counter-attack on his critics, *Casual Condemnations*, gave the impression that all the critics had been hostile to *The Friends*, whereas opinions were divided enough for him to run a advertisement quoting alternate good and bad reviews (five of each) towards the end of the run; but unfortunately many of the hostile critics were from the more influential journals – such as Frank Marcus of the *Sunday Telegraph*, who objected to the detectable presence of Wesker and his ideas in the play: 'It is a requiem for seven voices, all of them Wesker's'. This was not everyone's impression, but was lent apparent credibility from the fact that Wesker directed the play himself.

There had been very positive responses from those who read the text in the winter of 1968–69 – Terry Hands called it 'An extraordinarily moving and frightening elegy' and William Gaskill wrote 'I wanted to say straight away that I would like it to be done here [the Royal Court]', while Martin Esslin said 'I found the play very moving and stimulating and also very interesting indeed' (TQ 2 p. 79). (These impressions of the text coincide with only a few of the reviews of the actual production.) Wesker however replied to interested directors: 'I must tell you that the wish to direct it myself is growing more strong and I don't think I am going to let the play be done unless I can direct it'. The subsidized theatres were not prepared to concede this, so *The Friends* ended up at the Roundhouse, backed by ship-owner Eddie Kulukundis. Garry O'Connor published his diary account of the rehearsal period, feeling 'a duty to record something of this baroque event' though the story 'in its entirety is perhaps better left untold'. As he said, 'a period of rehearsal prior to an opening is a period of acute difficulty and tension, and many of the comments – harsh at the time – should not now be taken too seriously' (TQ 2 p. 78), but it seems to have been a rather more painful than average production process.

One fundamental and perhaps inevitable point of conflict was Wesker's usual wish to recreate the play as near as possible to how he had conceived it; he saw his plays as continuing to evolve through the first production, but not changing radically in, say, matters of interpretation of character. The basic concept of the play in performance, including the interpretation of the characters and how they relate to each other, Wesker felt should be his domain and his alone, and the contribution of the cast to this should be executive and not substantial: 'to co-operate with actors in finding the best production approach to that concept, yes, that's natural, and inherent in the theatre anyway' (TQ 28 p. 16). The problem came with drawing the line between where a 'production approach' started to alter the author's basic concept. At the first read-through Wesker noted 'the extent to which they were *wrong* in their reading' (TQ 2 p. 82) [my italics], and although, particularly in a play of this kind, the characters have to balance, contrast, interact in a certain way or their reactions to each other cease to relate properly, Wesker's approach to 'right' and 'wrong' readings suggests more absolutism than his 'co-operate' statement does. A tug of war for dominance ensued, and though Wesker's first notes had specified 'there comes a final moment for decision and I will both decide when that moment comes and what that moment's decision is' (TQ 2 p. 81), in practice he seems to have been decisive chiefly about interpretation. Susan Engel thought his very definitive character notes were 'rammed down your throat', and to Garry O'Connor they 'refuse[d] life and the element of chance' (TQ 2 p. 85). In other respects Wesker was only too flexible: O'Connor noted 'the situation of this play has been entirely reversed from that of any other I have been involved with, for the actors appear entirely to dominate it with their needs' (TQ 2 p. 89), and the designer Georgiadis recommended a touch of the jackboot:

> The cast think he treats them like dirt. The extraordinary thing is that Arnold doesn't treat them like dirt. He treats them like equals: they want to be treated like dirt – part of the time at least. They really want to be treated like children. To be loved, and – the ultimate of indulgence – to believe all the good ideas you give them are their own imagination. We should install a nursery ... You should understand not to play their

games. Surely everyone can see through the kissing and hugging. Don't they know their Freud? It is deep-rooted aggression. (TQ 2 p. 92)

There *was* some very deep-rooted aggression at work, grounded on the different positions of actors and author-director, especially in the case of Victor Henry, a brilliant young actor who played Roland and who saw acting as 'gladiatorial'. His philosophy was totally and destructively opposed to Wesker's, particularly as embodied in *The Friends*: the 'first great myth of all time – the creation of order out of chaos' was anathema to him. A Canadian student, Norma Levine, who visited the rehearsals described Henry as

> an actor in whom burn all the fires of anarchy, the incarnation of a character constantly creating his own play, the kind of actor other actors are fascinated by, find brilliant, and ultimately respect. He's been called psychotic, brilliant, diabolic. And when he speaks, spasmodic outbursts of uncontrolled, twisted energy with frequently interpolated crudities, they become still and respectful. Partly fascination. Partly terror. On his body he carries a sharp dagger and they think he'll use it at the right moment. He resembles nothing so much as a mass of energy in the scientific sense. It can be put to either good or evil, creation or destruction, but there is no moral principle that governs the decision. Except perhaps this: 'No one has the right to be vulnerable' he has said. Grandly he has announced his intent to destroy Arnold Wesker, who comes an unarmed powerless alien into his universe which makes no connection between cause and effect. (*Hakaveret*, Vol. I, no. 3, p. 11)

O'Connor's opinion was that Wesker got too involved with his actors' personal lives, took too much of an interest instead of maintaining a distance that would support his authority. (In Sweden, where Wesker had directed the world première of *The Friends*, these problems had not arisen, whether because none of the cast was particularly difficult to deal with, or whether because the language barrier had established the necessary distance – and respect.) O'Connor gives an account of one 'all-time low' in rehearsals:

> one scene deteriorates into a mixture of black farce and gladiatorial cruelty, with Victor telling Wesker he is a bad director. Not too bad – he gets marks for trying – but ultimately 'We all have the right to fail'. Victor, like Antony refusing to read the will in *Julius Caesar*, leaves the rehearsal room three times and has to be implored to come back ... (TQ 2 p. 87)

90

At another point the actors refused to listen to Wesker's notes, and later the stage manager, Kulukundis and Ian Holm called on O'Connor to ask him to take over the direction, which he refused to do. This unhappy atmosphere was all the more distressing given that Wesker had initially invited the company to a house party in his Welsh cottage in the interest of creating a good *rapport*. (In fact one actor, James Bolam, succumbed to the gladiatorial element straightaway, and resigned before the visit was over.) Not surprising, then, that Wesker should have been disappointed in the end product – 'it does very little credit to him, to the cast, or to the play. It was, at both previews, a hundred times better' (TQ 2 p. 92), O'Connor recalled.

Asked whether he regretted having insisted on directing the play himself, Wesker replied: 'Obviously it was wrong because it didn't work out. But whether it was because I decided to direct it, or because I had decided to take on Victor Henry, or because I didn't get rid of him after two weeks – that's another question' (TQ 28 p. 8).

11

Watershed

> I was forty years old and had been writing for sixteen years. Two new plays were to appear under the wing of our major companies. A reputation was going to be consolidated. THE OLD ONES in May directed by John Dexter at the National Theatre, THE JOURNALISTS in the following October at the Aldwych. Neither play was performed by those companies. The year collapsed in ruins and heartache. What happened?[1]

These events of the early seventies pushed Wesker further into the non-establishment wilderness following his sixties detour into organizing Centre Fortytwo and lack of success – in England – of both *Four Seasons* and *Golden City*. These and *The Friends*, because of its valedictory Roundhouse production, came under the Centre Fortytwo shadow, whereas having plays staged by the big subsidized London companies, Wesker thought, would have brought him back into the fold of mainstream drama – not that, as will be seen later, it had quite that effect on his contemporary John Arden's career at this point. The difficulties of developing as a dramatist were as acute as they had been when Wesker had sent his furious 'we are just starting to write' letter to the *New Statesman* in 1959. Now, in 1974, Michael Billington put his finger on the problem of instant obsolescence:

> I was astonished when a very intelligent theatre-director said to me recently that the British theatre seemed dead at the moment in that no writers had emerged since Brenton, Hare and Snoo Wilson: the assumption apparently was that, just as the pop charts to stay alive have to discover new sounds, so the theatre was totally moribund unless a new wave of writers crashed on the beach-head each year. Of course, young talent is constantly needed; but the result of our insatiable craze for newness is that writers like Stoppard, Nichols and Storey are now branded as safe Establishment figures while Osborne, Pinter, Wesker and Arden are thought of as palaeolithic just when they are at an age when they should be producing their richest work.[2]

Unless a dramatist is going to write in exactly the style of each new wave as it comes along – very unlikely – then the only alternative ways of proceeding seem to be to keep on writing the same kind of very characteristic play – as Samuel Beckett does – or to follow his or her own possibly unfashionable line. *The Friends*, in spite of many good reviews, had not had the immediate dramatic impact of *Chips*, but it was a different type of play altogether, and could not wipe out the coolness with which the previous two plays had been received. The whole experience had shaken Wesker's confidence, as he said in a *Guardian* interview: 'I don't think I've quite recovered from that disastrous production of *The Friends* in London. It was the director's fault – my fault. I allowed the actors to be terrorized by one other actor.'[3]

The Old Ones was to be directed by John Dexter, who had spent some years at the National Theatre.

> While John Dexter went on holiday, Kenneth Tynan – then literary manager of the National Theatre – took the unilateral decision to withdraw *The Old Ones* from the scheduled programme. (He told me later he didn't think it could be cast from their company. Not a decision for him to make!) I made representations to Arnold Goodman, the Chairman of the Arts Council, who advised me to see a lawyer while he made representations to Sir Max Rayne, Chairman of the National Theatre's board of trustees. Sir Laurence Olivier had second thoughts (if, to his credit, he ever shared first ones with Ken Tynan), and offered me a new date. But by this time John Dexter, deeply hurt to have been so cursorily treated after all the work he'd put into the building up of the company and its reputation, asked me to follow him and accept the offer of the Royal Court to direct the play in our old home. I agreed.[4]

Wesker also of course was hurt by this – he considered that 'the delivery of a play to a theatre that has contracted for it is a commitment of faith of such delicacy that to abuse it in any way is a kind of rape. Every artist will recognize the offering of their work not as the offering of something they have merely written but of themselves.'

The *Journalists* affair was less clear-cut – 'more complex and sinister'. In the first place, coincidentally it was preceded by a quite different but discouraging wrangle with certain journalists on the *Sunday Times* where Wesker had gone to spend two months on background research for his projected play. He 'couldn't resist shaping the notes ... into a piece of journalism' (JJ p. 6), secretly hoping to produce an inspired piece which the editor couldn't resist or felt challenged to print. Harold Evans, the editor of the

Sunday Times was able to resist it, but agreed to its publication by Cape subject to some rewriting of bits that he thought were biassed or inadequate. The contract was signed and the advance paid when certain journalists objected. The first complaint was that Wesker had gained their confidence under false pretences as he had been accepted as gathering material for a play, not an undisguised descriptive piece; and in addition there was quite a lot of hostility to the image that the essay projected – built on inaccuracies, it was thought. Eventually Wesker withdrew the manuscript and paid back his advance. Five years later in a television interview, Harold Evans implied that the book might as well now see the light of day: He turned to the camera and said 'You can go ahead and publish, Arnold,' (JJ p. 7). He had not personally objected to publication in the first place, and the remaining objectors were still objecting, but Wesker considered that his initial 'self-imposed' vow that 'I'd publish only if everyone with whom I'd spoken agreed' (JJ p. 7) had been reasonably honoured, and he published his 'slim volume'.

As his later notes show, the book was an invaluable source of material – 'I'm constantly dipping into the *Journey into Journalism* article for passages of dialogue and adding them into the play. That article is like a pool of reserves. I can use it for anything' (TQ 26 p. 7). His ear for dialogue had found plenty to record in the particular style and jargon of this profession; he was 'confused by the shorthand language they adopt to communicate ideas among themselves, and frequently overwhelmed by the incomprehensible technical vocabulary they call upon ...' (JJ p. 15), and at first he felt 'I can't hear what they're saying because I'm so absorbed by the way they're saying it' (JJ p. 12). But for all his admiration for the wit and intelligence of the journalists, Wesker came out no more reconciled to journalism than he went in – one of the reasons for the affronted reactions perhaps. He still saw journalism as a kind of privileged destructiveness:

> Yet, despite such disarming wit, I can't rid myself of the suspicion that they seem to *relish* the process of what they expose more than they *care* about what is exposed. A very dubious mechanism is at work when such a large number of people assume for themselves the self-righteous responsibility of interfering to protect society against others whom *they* have decided are interfering and self-righteous. Especially when their own definition of their duty to investigate 'secret and well-protected

94

misbehaviour' is such a boomerang. Journalism may not be a secret activity but it is certainly one of the most 'well-protected'. Which editor would allow an investigatory profile of his newspaper to appear in his own columns? (JJ p. 104).

Several reviews of the book noticed the irony of the journalists objecting to being on the receiving end of the sort of revealing investigation they did themselves. Tim Heald commented in *The Times*:

It's either very sad or very funny that their objections should so exactly mirror those of most journalists' victims: distortion, misrepresentation, lack of proper research and, above all, gaining the information under false pretences. You can almost hear them moaning: 'But he seemed such a nice young man. I thought he was on our side'.

But on the other hand the objections to partiality and inaccuracy – some of which were admitted and corrected – show Wesker in turn as guilty of what *he* disliked in journalism: exercising selective attention to detail. For instance, he had demonstrated the disarming honesty and modesty of the Insight team as they started from scratch inquiring into a subject they didn't know about, but the Insight people themselves thought that the description of their initial ignorance and elementary first approach had eclipsed everything else – 'what emerges is that Insight is a technically sloppy ... group of half-wits'. And this was because Wesker himself didn't know the whole story:

My original draft relies mostly on observation. I *hear* them making jokes about fallen bridges – I don't *see* them ploughing through reports. I *hear* them phoning around for information – I don't *see* them in consultation with technical advisers. (JJ p. 24)

Naturally the reviewers of the account, being journalists themselves took sides very decidedly in this affair. Atticus of the *Sunday Times*, recounting that 'There are those, I am told, who polished their aphorisms for hours before going off to bump into him in the pub', summed the book up as 'an amusing and well heard, if incomplete, picture of a random group of journalists attempting to do their jobs whilst a playwright is in the room watching them'.

How seriously had Wesker taken the role-playing element? He thought that he had made allowance for this. 'At the beginning there certainly was a lot of hyping for my benefit, but finally they had to do their work' (TQ 28 p. 14). Another *Sunday Times* critic, Anthony Howard, felt he 'is at times irreverent but more often he is simply wide-eyed: in fact something of a star-struck tone pervades the whole narrative'. Richard Hoggart in *New Society* was more suspicious: 'One gets the impression here that Arnold Wesker sees himself as a sort of open-eyed Candide figure ... So much so that one sometimes feels like scribbling in the margin: "Come off it, Arnold, you're not as innocent as all that",' a view shared by Richard Clements of *Tribune*; in a similar observer situation Clements had found Wesker 'naive to the point of embarrassment' until 'I started to realize that it was not so much naivety, but technique'. The consensus seemed to be that, wide-eyed or not, the much-quoted imprimatur of the late Nick Tomalin had been earned: 'You got it as right as any of us ever get anything right!'

The bones of contention here – whether material had been gathered under false pretences, and whether the picture given was accurate – did not have anything to do with more important conflict over the play *The Journalists*. The crux of the matter at the Royal Shakespeare Company was that the actors did not like the play. Their objections mainly stemmed from their lack of conviction about the play, both as a play ('no climaxes, emotional relationships, human contact or throughlines') and in its subject matter ('did not ring true as an image of press life'). One can set against these views respectively the later successful amateur production, and the judgment of professional journalists themselves; but the actors' rejection of the play was decisive, as a majority had a 'right-to-refuse' clause in their contracts and, rightly or wrongly, believed that they would not be able to do both *The Journalists* and the concurrently planned play by John Arden and Margaretta D'Arcy, *The Island of the Mighty*.

It may seem odd that a management and director, having contracted for a play, should be brought up short by the cast at such a late stage. (If democracy is going to operate, it should surely be built in at an earlier part of the process.) The basic error seems to have been to leave the play to sink or swim without an advocate: David Jones, a friend of Wesker's, had commissioned the play and was to direct it, but he went on holiday leaving the casting to Maurice Daniels, who in turn was overworked before his own holiday and passed it on to a director who was not involved in the play, John Barton.

96

The resulting turmoil and uncertainty led to the play's not appearing in the booking schedule as arranged. The artistic director, Trevor Nunn, took over responsibility and proposed a rewrite for production at the RSC's small Stratford auditorium, The Other Place. To Wesker The Other Place was a space for students to play around in. He disliked it, thinking it looked defeated and dull, too small for *The Journalists* and seemed short on adequate technical resources. After an angry exchange of letters, Wesker wrote to Nunn:

> You have a right not to like *The Journalists*: the actors have the right not to want to perform in it; David Jones has the right to cool off a play; and it is no crime to have mismanaged affairs as you described it to me when we met so that the wrong person offered the roles to the actors ... I understand all that. But who is to pay for all these shifts and failings?[5]

But finally, refusing The Other Place offer, Wesker filed a suit against the RSC for breach of contract. Wesker:

> The case dragged on till November 1980 when a settlement was reached paying me £4250, £2400 of which went in legal fees. The RSC's lawyers did what all good defence lawyers must do, they left every stage of the action till the last possible minute, sometimes even beyond, and threw in every possible – and impossible – scrap of paper to make progress heavy-going.[6]

By ironic comparison, the Arden/D'Arcy play, which the company had found 'marvellous, magnificent, mythic, poetic', went into rehearsal under better auspices, but in this case the authors felt that the end product was a distortion of what had been intended as an anti-imperialist play. A notorious public fracas ensued, in which the authors picketed the theatre. Wesker recalled that 'They asked me to support them. I thought their stand was an emotional one and would make them appear ridiculous ... I advised them to take legal action and call for an injunction to prevent the play opening'. Nonetheless, recounting John Arden's frustrated attempt to explain his position to the first-night audience, Wesker quotes Arden's valedictory words 'In that case, I will leave this theatre and never write one word for you again', and wondered how many of his fellow-dramatists had felt the urge to utter the same renunciation.

Apart from the obvious irony of the fate of the Arden/D'Arcy play, the experience of these dramatists supports Wesker's increasing suspicion of playwrights' 'abuses and betrayals which seem to characterize their relationship with their profession's other members'. Later, in 1974, Nigel Lewis in the *Guardian* referred back not only to the *Island of the Mighty* dispute but to Pinter's wholesale condemnation of Visconti's production of *Old Times* (see p. 16) and asked Wesker why he had not resisted, for instance, Gaskill's and Dexter's agreement that there should not be separate sets of old and young characters in *Golden City*. Wesker explained that it was partly because he hadn't the power, the play having passed out of his hands, partly because of a phenomenon which he described in the *Plays and Players* article (February 1974), namely 'suggestions for changes in text, characterization, emphasis or rhythm which seem perfectly sensible but which are wrong for *reasons the author has forgotten*'. It is this sort of ambivalence that made Arden and D'Arcy hesitate until too late before finally disagreeing with their director. 'This kind of recalcitrance on the playwright's part stems from his awareness of the complexity of the play, and his desire not to interfere with the director's attempt to engage with it'.[7] It is an extension of every dramatist's problem: that his concept of the play is not wholly contained in the text, and that until realized on stage as he saw it in his mind's eye – or, with revisions, has come to see it – the play has not reached its final form. Small wonder that the dramatist tends to be touchy and possessive about his half-born progeny, and seems to aspire after the condition of Beethoven – composing the concerto, playing the solo and conducting from the keyboard. As Wesker tries to explain in an unpublished coda to his account of the RSC fiasco:

Why have I gone to such lengths to gather in the details of this story? After all, the actors and the others could be right, *The Journalists* could be an awful play. Perhaps yes, but perhaps not. I only know that the directors of the Royal Court theatre did not at first think my Trilogy could work, or *The Kitchen*, or *Chips With Everything*. Peggy Ashcroft rescued *Roots*, the late Bryan Bailey of the Belgrade Theatre in Coventry rescued *Chicken Soup with Barley*, John Dexter rescued *The Kitchen*, Bob Swash rescued *Chips With Everything*. There is a similar story to tell for all of my plays since, the majority can't 'hear' them until they are performed. When, I ask myself, will *my* experience, expertise, track-record, be trusted?

Small wonder, too, that by the 1980s both Arden and Wesker had started writing novels.

12

The Journalists and *The Old Ones*

The RSC actors, then, rejected Wesker's *The Journalists*, and he felt that its fate was depressingly ironic. In his introduction to the play he states firmly 'The *Kitchen* is not about cooking, it's about man and his relationship to work. *The Journalists* is not about journalism, it is about the poisonous human need to cut better men down to our size, from which need we all suffer in varying degrees' (IV 9), and he goes on to adapt from Swift the label 'Lilliputianism' for this need. Thus, he commented 'my play was about the lilliputian mentality, and the actors had responded in a lilliputian manner – they'd brought down a daring and ambitious play'.

It *is* an ambitious play, and Wesker was concerned to point out the development from his earlier work, especially *The Kitchen*, because at first sight they have many similarities:

> Both are attempts to organise experience. They both have other things in common as well, the form and the setting. Both have a large cast of about thirty who are on stage most of the time and both are set in a place of work: the kitchen of a huge restaurant; the offices of a large Sunday newspaper. They also have similar rhythms – *The Kitchen* begins with the chefs and waitresses slowly ambling into an empty space and preparing for a frenzied serving as the day reaches its climax. *The Journalists* begins at the beginning of the week and slowly moves towards the frenzied activity on a Saturday when the paper is being put to bed. [Unpublished lecture]

Apart from the nature of the experience being used, especially as Wesker had been behind the scenes as a professional cook, but had merely been a customer of journalism, the main difference lies between the two themes, work and lilliputianism, and the type of character who exemplifies those themes. In *The Journalists* the main character is Mary Mortimer, a combative columnist whose work ranges over personalities and social comment, and she is admired – or disliked – for her 'cool, witty and deadly' column which cuts down to size those whom she sees as pompous and self-important. '*That's* the function of journalism' she says, 'to

protect society from shabbly little charlatans like him' (*IV* 38) –
i.e. a newsworthy, idealistic MP, Morgan King. Mary's obsessive
feud with King provides only an unobtrusive linking story, just as
Peter's affair with Monique in *The Kitchen* surfaces only intermittently.

Mary is a lilliputianizing giant-killer, then; 'Don't you find
something irritating about a good person?' is one of her less
rational – or rationalized – remarks (swiftly demolished by
Tamara's 'It's perfectly easy to identify: their goodness, by com-
arison, reveals our shabbiness' (*IV* 50)). But her 'order out of
chaos' speech shows that she is close to taking the responsible
view herself. The speech is a defence against her grown-up children's accusation of being 'bourgeois', and there are reminiscences
of Simone's argument for values and against chaos here:

> I'm not bourgeois if I acknowledge a debt to dead men and if I'm fearful
> about the future. That's human. To *enjoy* being helpless about evil
> *that's* bourgeois, but to *feel*, to just simply *feel* helpless about evil that's
> human. To have loves and hates and failures and regrets and nostalgias,
> that's human. If I pretend order exists when it doesn't *that's* bourgeois,
> but if I try to create order out of the chaos of my miserable life that's
> human, bloody human, bloody bloody human. (*IV* 69)

But before she enters, her children have been reading out an extract
from her column attacking Morgan King's belief that 'the first
great myth of all time was the story of the creation of order out of
chaos' (*IV* 65), and as her daughter Agnes says 'You see, mother,
he also talks about order out of chaos'. That's just what we mean.
It's as though you're fighting yourself' (*IV* 70). Her double standard has already been noted by John: 'She can't bear idealism
anywhere but in her own column, where she calls it "responsibility", whereas in anyone else's it's called "charlatanism"'
(*IV* 62).

It is interesting here, as in *The Friends*, to compare the working
out of Wesker's concern with values with that in *Roots*. Mary is
an anti-Beatie in that she is a whirlwind of trigger-happy articulacy
throughout the play until at the end the shock of having her
scoop ignored virtually silences her – at least for once destroys
her assurance. And like Ronnie, Mary's off-stage antagonist,
Morgan King, never appears in person. He too is very much of a
mouthpiece for Arnold Wesker – some of the speeches attributed

to King come from Wesker's other works, such as the 'patterns men can make for the pleasure of their living' (*IV* 60), which is a quotation from *Golden City* (*II* 188). This becomes a little self-indulgent where Wesker takes the opportunity to answer criticisms that had been aimed at himself, such as the post-Centre Fortytwo 'You're taking culture to the masses!', which Sebastian neatly fields with 'as though to *take* anything to people were somehow more sinister than to *sell* it to them. Capital fellow!' (*IV* 63). King is not an artist, and is not 'taking' culture anywhere, and his role as spokesman for the artist sits awkwardly on him.

Morgan King is associated with a further weakness in the whole argument of the play. As Mary has suspected, there *is* something odd about him, and a lucky guess and an informer with documents give her proof that he has not just been talking about Jerusalem, but is actively involved with a quixotic band of urban guerrillas who raid banks to support a justified strike and rob supermarkets to give goods to old-age pensioners. And the backhander that makes the editor suppress her revelation is another journalist's discovery that her own younger son Jonathan is one of King's masked band. Thus, Mary is, as Agnes had warned her, fighting against herself in more ways than one.

Mary's near-miss at bringing down her enemy and unwittingly also her son is thematically appropriate. As Wesker initially worked it out, Morgan King 'is still shown to be an idealistic side of herself with which she is uneasy and feels a constant need to attack' (TQ 26 p. 7), and her children personify that idealistic element in her (originally he planned to have all three as members of the secret society). But compared with the careful authenticity and naturalism of the rest of the play ('I almost can't bring myself to let a character say "OK" ... I must force myself to accept that I've chosen an ultra-naturalistic setting' (TQ 26 p. 8)) this winding up of the feud is melodramatic. Wesker had earlier eliminated scenes actually showing the secret society confronting another 'Angry Brigade' group, because he'd never felt happy with them: 'I don't believe a word of it. I'm not really good at introducing thriller-type plots into my plays' (TQ 26 p. 7) and had worried about the melodrama of the conclusion too. The *effect* of melodrama is modified by its being absorbed and taken over by the sound and film of the print machines turning out the paper, but the thriller element disrupts the naturalism and undermines the lilliputianism of the message: that lilliputianizing is the destructiveness of cutting better men down to size.

David Nathan, reviewing the text, suggests that 'Wesker's idea of the "better men" would not go unchallenged by anyone, much less a group of investigative journalists and columnists'. This is a fair comment. If Morgan King is one of the better men, what is he doing at the head of an illegal, in fact a criminal organization? And if he doesn't believe in legality, why is he an MP? Asked about this, Wesker replied

> I've always been aware of this as a potential weakness and at one time I had a justification for it though – God help me! – I've forgotten now what it is! I think it was something to do with not wanting to load the dice against Mary. She was right, but the wrong person to be right. It was also self-destructive in that she brings down her son. I can't quite put my finger on it but it nags at me that it would be wrong to have her be wrong about Morgan King. Nevertheless I shall think more about it.

Mary's complicated motives, her excuses and self-deception, the analysis and criticism from her colleagues, can be expressed far more fully than the reactions of the semi-articulate cooks of *The Kitchen*, even though the lilliputianizing theme can be traced back to Paul's account of the bus-driver who literally wanted to cut down the do-gooders protest-marching in the way of his bus. 'Twelve years on I was looking for lilliputians in much loftier places than the ranks of poor beleaguered bus-drivers', Wesker points out, and the media people of *The Journalists* are perfectly capable of articulating all kinds of social problems, their own and other people's.

The play's title had originally been in the singular – *The Journalist* – and Wesker later decided to make it plural to avoid suggesting that it was only about Mary, and much of the action shows her colleagues working, dealing with news items, relaxing, in conference, and so on. Mary's children tell her that her 'only contribution to British journalism is to have elevated the gutter question "who does he think he is?" to a respected art form' (IV 90) – a phrase she uses twice about Morgan King. The other journalists make their contribution by trivializing issues, building up nonentities into sages and levelling all variety in the flow of news to the same dead blandness. D. A. N. Jones described them as 'quite witty, thoughtful, smart and terribly upset'. If not upset, exactly, the characters are quite aware of their predicament. Early in the play, two journalists Cynthia and Norman discuss a photographer colleague:

> When he first came here he could hardly talk. Just threw his photographs on the desk and asked could we use them? ... Even then he had an eye for violence and desolation and waste, but his work has turned this into an obsession: And I can't get him to snap anything else now. 'Where the violence is, send me there' he says. And he's right. He can't photograph peace. And it's our fault. (*IV* 24–5)

Then we see Tamara, a foreign correspondent, sinking gradually into a nervous breakdown. 'What in the world is worth such savage slaughter ... Cut it? I want to weep on it' (*IV* 29) she says, and her colleague Gordon comments: 'She worries me. She's speaking louder, faster and, with her deep-throated Slavic accent, she's becoming like a Noël Coward caricature' (*IV* 32). By the end of the play she gives way: 'I don't think I can really cope much more, Gordon' (*IV* 101). The last straw has been the massacre of doctors, professors, writers and teachers in a foreign war which she links with their own lilliputianizing – 'it's Mary's "who-does-he-think-he-is?" gone insane'. But Tamara's reaction is the exception. Gordon remarks briskly 'For Christ's sake you're a journalist. Is this any worse than your reports on the Eichmann trial?' and adds 'Men have been slaughtering their thinkers for centuries' (*IV* 101). Most journalists have to develop a certain shell, Richard Clements argued, quoting Bernard Shaw's opinion that journalists and publicans should not get too involved in their work:

> Publicans would end up drunkards and journalists so involved with the feelings of those whom they wrote about that they could no longer put pen to paper. That problem Wesker put his finger on – and he does it in such a brilliant fashion that everyone who has been involved in journalism must feel the pain.

He was discussing *Journey into Journalism*, but in the play the effect is if anything more pronounced. And then comes the problem that the newspaper's readers, bombarded with atrocities, develop a similar carapace: the news itself is lilliputianized.

But, as Mary herself says in one of her few long speeches, it is a human aspiration to create order out of chaos, and this levelling down of people and issues to an indistinguishable mass is merely creating more chaos out of chaos. Thus Arts-page journalists Sebastian and John analyse this contradiction between Mary's theory and practice, 'She can't bear people who make judgments, and since in attacking them, *she* has to judge, therefore she's torn all ends up ... If you make a judgment you seem, by your choice, to be indicting those who've not chosen as you've done (*IV* 62). This point is taken up in Mary's later important interview with Chancellor of the Exchequer Sir Reginald MacIntyre, who says 'Supposing all our judgments are wrong? Yours of me, mine of you? – so? Do we cease making them?' (*IV* 72). Cynthia sums up the chaotic result of withholding judgement:

> Don't you ever feel uneasy, sometimes, as a journalist? We inundate people with depressing information and they become concerned. Then we offer more information and they become confused. And then we pile on more and more until they feel impotent but we offer them no help. No way out of their feelings of impotence. Don't you ever feel guilty? [*IV* 43]

What Cynthia says about the piles of information is exactly what Manfred's complaint about new knowledge in *The Friends* – some system of evaluating all this is essential, and the need to fill up space leads to superficial *ad hoc* priorities. Some priorities are necessary, as there is limited space to be filled, but those of the journalists can not only level out but cast a false emphasis on the story presented. At the end of the play Jane (from the Women's Pages) and Dominic (of Business News) propose a slogan, on the lines of the government health notice on cigarette packets: 'Warning! the selective attention to detail herein contained may warp your view of the world!' (*IV* 110). But as Michael Billington pertinently asked, isn't the alternative to selectivity unselectivity? And that has been rejected too. Ultimately, one must select – but responsibly, by making judgements.

A minor problem with the play is the topicality of the newspaper material in the printed text. Massacres and famines are always with us, as Gordon assures Tamara, but some items of news, such as the Russian astronauts dying in space, were events of a certain year, and 'date' correspondingly. This can hardly help the play's increasingly remote chances of a professional production in its own country; but for performances abroad, Wesker carefully cut out any references that could be tied to a particular year.

105

While *The Journalists* was being disputed over by the RSC, Wesker had withheld foreign productions, and initial enquirers lost interest as the legal wrangle wore on. The first professional production eventually took place in German in Wilhelmshaven in 1981. Previously there had been an amateur production at the Criterion Theatre Coventry, a two-day student production at Lancaster Arts Festival, and French and Jugoslavian productions adapted for radio and television respectively – one way of making it easier to deal with over thirty characters and over a hundred brief scenes, some only three lines long, which make up the mosaic panorama of the play. Wesker himself was fairly casual about the problems he was setting his directors:

> ... because I don't see that they are as difficult as you suggest. Just as *The Kitchen* didn't seem to me to be difficult to stage as I wrote it, and then before the production everybody said how difficult it would be – yet when we actually put it on in two weeks, somehow it all fell into place. I think that after a while one learns to trust one's instincts. In *The Journalists* it's only that you've got more people to keep occupied, and at the same time keep quiet, while something else is going on. That's not impossible – a straightforward theatrical problem. (TQ 28 p. 14)

At the end of the first week at the *Sunday Times* Wesker had got the idea of how his original themes and the actual dramatic material he was gathering were going to come together: 'It must be set like *The Kitchen*, all departments on stage at once, the story weaving its way from one group to another', and ideally, 'to the rear of the stage, a large screen of the machine which, as the end approaches, slowly begin to move and spit out the sheets of newsprint with its attendant noise in the background' (JJ pp. 45–6). The original playtext published by the Writers and Readers Cooperative included Hayden Griffin's sketches for a set, though Wesker was not, for once, prescriptive about the design:

> it's actually all very clearly dictated, because you have eight areas, so that you know that the three-dimensional box which is the stage in front of you has to be split up into eight areas, where a simultaneous action is always taking place, and one ninth area, which is utilized only when the rest is in darkness. Now, whether you do it in the way that Hayden Griffin laid it out, or whether you have a series of imagined boxes with stairs going from one to another, set at different levels, it has to be something like that. My only strict requirement for the set

was that the action must be able to shift from office to office, but not adjacent ones. Concentration had to move from extreme ends of the stage, otherwise it would become boring. There would have to be some juggling to ensure that. But that seemed to me the only problem the play set: the rest was a matter of choreography, of moving actors around – fun for the director. (TQ 28 p. 15)

Michael Billington at the Coventry production congratulated Bob Morley and Terry Nichols who had 'on the tiny Criterion stage, managed to build an astonishing desk-cluttered set', and the 'slowly accelerating pace' worked too. Evidently a competent amateur director could bring off this complex staging, as Geoff Bennett did here (though an American amateur production was damned with faint praise for 'keeping the pace up and the people from stumbling all over one another on the small stage' – even the negative implies confusion enough). And for the sake of the particular dramatic effect he wanted, Wesker had rejected compactness quite consciously: 'One could have written a play exploring the minimalizing theme in the way that, say, *Front Page* worked – in just one room' (TQ 28 p. 14):

And I was very aware of the special effect which could be created by juxtaposing one issue alongside another. That special effect, that juxta-positioning is what I call poetry in the theatre and it's indefinable. You can only place two passages alongside one another and trust it works for an audience, rather like editing a film and placing the images alongside one another. The correct juxtaposing of two objects in a room is called harmony, their relationship is pleasing. If you place two statements alongside each other so that, though unrelated, yet they intensify each other then that's what I think can be called poetic. [Unpublished lecture]

Poetry was just what the RSC actors had not found in their first reading of the script, but when it finally reached the small stage at Coventry, Michael Billington concluded that 'there is no denying the plays originality of form or richness of content ... The Criterion's coup is the professional theatre's shame.'

THE OLD ONES

I suppose it's as simple as that I had an enormous admiration for my mother and her cronies, her band of extraordinary old ladies. Sarah is the still centre, surrounded by these extraordinary old people who find all sorts of ways to survive and carry on ... I don't think I can say any more except that I'm full of admiration for all the relatives, aunts and uncles, who are mixed into the play – a very extraordinary collection of tough personalities who were good and vivid, and seemed to make significant patterns. (TQ 28 p. 11)

No special research was needed for *The Old Ones* as it covers familiar Wesker territory, and virtually extends the Trilogy into a quartet; Wesker adds 'You can imagine that all the old ones in all the plays are the same people' (TQ 28 p. 11). For instance the Sarah of this play, based as he says on his mother, is therefore very like the Sarah of the Trilogy, if a little mellower – either with less fight in her or with less to fight about. The setting is the flat-dwelling neighbourhood where the old people live, rather as in the last acts of *Chicken Soup*, but the mood is less defeated. This Sarah no longer has a paralysed and incontinent husband to cope with, her daughter Rosa lives near enough to visit her frequently, and she 'always has a tea with people, always full with people' (*III* 158). Almost all the characters are Jewish, though this is not necessarily connected with the theme of toughness and survival. Most of them are also related, including Sarah's brothers, Manny and Boomy, Boomy's wife Gerda and his son Martin, Sarah's daughter Rosa, another nephew Rudi. Teressa and Millie are Sarah's friends, and her neighbour Jack is the only gentile among her cronies.

Yet curiously Wesker had 'an old-fashioned blockage' about writing this play – curiously, because of the familiarity of the material, but then again perhaps not so curious after the hiatus of the Centre Fortytwo period and his dissatisfaction with the fate of the previous three plays *The Four Seasons*, *Golden City* and *The Friends*. Then, before embarking on *The Old Ones*, he had written the unpublished, possibly libellous *New Play*:

And accompanying this blockage was this urge not to write plays in the old way. I was tired of the ordinary stage, with actors coming on and off and sets being changed, and with inventing slightly different characters with different names. So I decided to let it all hang out, as they say. Everybody in that play [*The New Play*] is called by their real name. There is a character called Arnold, there is a character called Leah, who is my mother, there are characters who are my mother's friends, there are characters of Jennie Lee, Robert Maxwell, Harold Lever – people who were involved in Centre Fortytwo – and my wife Dusty, and so on.

Because they all seemed to come together and form a part of my experience which was blocking me. I was paralysed, crippled. So in terms of character and name, everyone was who they were. In terms of technical structure, I used just about everything – slides, film, the magic lantern. I recorded my mother talking about her early years and I planned that the play would open with her voice being heard, actually talking in that halting way that émigrés have. And that would fade into the actress who was playing the character. And there would be these sepia photographs – which I finally used on the poster for *The Friends* – of my relatives. (TQ 28 p. 10)

Quite different from *The Old Ones*, *The New Play* nonetheless served as a quarry for some of the dialogue – for instance Sarah's reluctance to accept her daughter's gift of liqueurs is based on a scene in the earlier play between 'Arnold' and his mother.

Where *The New Play*, though roughly shaped by four 'circles of perception', is otherwise fairly chaotic and associative in development, *The Old Ones* is carefully patterned. Yet a common criticism from reviewers was, as B. A. Young put it, that 'It has no plot at all except insofar as the chart of a community's emotions may be called a plot. It has no protagonist, unless a community may be called a protagonist', and while John Barber called it 'a play that leaves one emotionally extended' he nonetheless wished that 'instead of an album of snapshots, Wesker had provided a story'. Michael Billington was sufficiently struck by the 'continuing quest for non-narrative theatre' to devote an article to a phenomenon he had noticed in several other recent plays, 'the slow, painful birth of a new kind of dramatic structure based more on music and poetry' though ' "new" is, of course, hardly the word since Chekhov's plays are all symphonic in structure'. Without going back as far as Chekhov, these complaints perhaps show merely the usual critical amnesia: Rosemary Say specifically detected a 'determination to break away from the strictly narrative format of such plays as *Roots*' and Felix Barker 'longed for the dramatic clarity and drive of his early plays', whereas it will be remembered that much criticism of *Roots* had centred on the fact that *nothing happened* until the very end. Wesker pointed out in an open letter replying to Harold Hobson's hostile review: 'you seem not to have noticed that I haven't used plots from the start – what is the plot of *The Kitchen*?'

But the *structure* of *The Old Ones* is surely in evidence from the beginning, and is based on the dialectic between the optimistic and pessimistic brothers, manic Manny and gloomy Boomy. They are involved in one of those eccentric rituals that grow up within families, a quotation competition, in which each seeks to confront the other with the ultimate, the irrefutable quotation to prove that life is either good or bad. In the first scene Manny quotes Yeats, Boomy replies, unseen, from his room, with Carlyle; in scene two, Martin imitates Boomy quoting Ecclesiastes, and Rosa retorts by reading out a benevolent anecdote about the founder of Hasidism; and the third scene is actually a monologue by Teressa alone in her flat, but as the lights dim we hear Boomy and Manny in voice-over swapping extracts from Ecclesiastes and Martin Buber. Boomy doesn't actually appear in person until the eighth scene, where he makes a highly theatrical entrance; he begins a rebuttal of Manny's cheerful Voltaire extract with his usual off-stage de-clamation, but half-way through 'enters, book in hand, declaiming in a mock histrionic voice', and walks slowly round them as he reads out a devastating list of plagues and earthquakes concluding ' "recall all *you* have suffered, admit that evil exists, and do not add to so many miseries and horrors the wild absurdity of denying them". (*Pause.*) Voltaire' (*III* 151). Thereafter we do not see Manny and Boomy in confrontation again until the long last scene, the party in Sarah's flat, but the voice of one or the other is heard in quotation at the end of several scenes. These quotations are tangentially relevant to the scenes they conclude, and *all* the scenes are tangentially relevant to the conflict between optimism and pessimism. Teressa expounds the tragic life of the poetess she is translating, while finding her own saving occupation in the process of translation; Sarah has her friends to tea; three youths attack Gerda; Jack strikes up a friendship with Millie; Martin is arrested for activities connected with student politics. Light and shade, family snapshots – but focussed by the urgency of the brothers' debate: does this show that life is after all worth living? Does that prove that men are irredeemably evil? Underlying the duel of quotations is the anxiety of the old men to take stock before it is too late, and justify their own lives; and the play itself is taking part in the debate.

The quotation battle also masks a personal rancour between the brothers, at least on Boomy's side. Manny in a fit of youthful idealism had rejected the idea of monetary advantage and thrown into the Thames the bag of uncut diamonds intended to finance their education – a substantial enough cause for resentment, admittedly. The rancour has become a habit – Boomy is even surprised that Gerda troubles to comment on it: 'I thought the worst was over. We don't scream like we used to. It's only a ritual that's left. Funny, even' (*III* 163). But apart from their relationship, the battle reveals deep-seated personal needs: the impulse to take stock in their old age is different for each of them. Manny is not convinced of goodness, but desperate to be convinced. He begins the play with his pre-dawn howl of despair launched at an empty universe: 'No light and no one there. Nothing . . . There should be an echo, a coming back or something' (*III* 133). And later he remarks hopefully that perhaps there will be 'On every headline in every newspaper, all over the world – something to reassure us'. Like so many of Wesker's characters he is crying out against chaos and contradictions, and looking for some magic, ready-made solution, preferably in print. Boomy on the other hand is using his philosophy of doom as a cover for his own defeat. His speech on the motives for violence – 'Self-knowledge that he's a pig and then – everything intimidates him . . . Hit it! Smash it! He'll show who's superior and who's not' (*III* 188) – is a self-indictment. His own self-knowledge that he has achieved nothing makes him hate achievement, and he reacts, if not with violence, with verbal destruction. As Macey in *The Friends* has said, it is better to

> avoid building up those little heavyweight philosophies about man and the world out of my own personal disappointments; to avoid confusing self-hatred with hatred of all men; to face the fact that though I'd failed, others hadn't. (*III* 113)

And Manny echoes this more forcefully: '*He's* made no impression on the world? So! It's a flat and dreary world. *He's* failed to live a life he can respect? So! It's a vain life' (*III* 192). Boomy remains entrenched in his despair, but at the end of the play Manny breaks out of the quotation rut, and this provides the climax towards which the strands of positive and negative experience have been leading throughout the action. As Manny's 'newspaper' remark hints, he is defending his need for reassurance at one remove, vicariously, from scraps of other people's opinions. The unenlightened Beatie Bryant was accused of 'quotin' all the time' (*I* 139), and Gerda urges Manny 'Say two words of your own to each other ... Yell at him in your own voice for a change' (*III* 150).

As far as fraternal relations are concerned, direct confrontation doesn't seem to produce any improvement, but Manny moves on from castigating Boomy for self-indulgence to evolving 'an original thought' – he invents a definition of cruelty that makes it comprehensible and so containable: 'cruelty is when one man is trying to create a situation in which *he* is not suffering pain' (*III* 191). Boomy quotes 'there is no new thing under the sun' back at him, but Manny has now, like Beatie, made a breakthrough. He goes on to offer an extended 'quotation' on the necessity to make one's contribution to the world, which concludes

> EMANUEL: 'If all action seems vain, must we cease all action ... he has no choice. The chef, the architect, the man of reason, do what they must because men must apply what is in them to apply. And so –'
> BOOMY: And so, and so?
> EMANUEL: 'And so, to cry "vanity of vanities" at foolish or evil men and then to abandon your true work is to abandon not them but yourself; it is to be guilty of an even greater vanity: for you knew what they did not.' (*III* 193)

Again this is familiar ground: it is the gist of Sarah Kahn's 'I should give up electricity?' speech, with further examples drawn from the territory inhabited by *The Kitchen* and *Golden City*. Dancing there at the party, naked except for his bath towel, the bare forked animal, the thing itself, Manny proclaims that his 'quotation' was his own unaided effort. Articulate at last, one might say. But more significantly, relying on his own (naked) worth and value at last. B. A. Young was irritated by the bath-and-towel presentation, which he found an irrelevant, out-of-character and unnecessary gimmick, but there are three answers on different levels: first, the bath has been prepared for, and is used by Manny as an excuse for stamping off in a sulk after a quarrel with Gerda; secondly, there is a jokey parallel, not explicit and therefore presumably not noticed by the critics, with Archimedes, that other discoverer of illumination in the bath ('I got it! I got it!' (*III* 190)); thirdly, Manny's near nakedness reflects his final rejection of borrowed robes, other men's thoughts.

So the final tableau of the Royal Court production ended with

Dexter's 'very *Fiddler on the Roof* image, with the revolve going one way and the cast dancing the other' (TQ 28 p. 12), dominated by Max Wall's cheeky Manny, which could be compared with the ending of *Roots* where Beatie's triumph overshadows her unregenerate family. But Wesker himself wanted to avoid the simplifying effect of a too positive ending: 'the ending I had envisaged ... was of a triangle of tensions between a group singing in the background and a brother who is hurling quotations of doom from Ecclesiastes and the brother he is hurling them at who is laughing' (TQ 28 p. 11). The last speech is Boomy's and is all quotation, and, in the revised text, goes on repeating insistently its message of despair:

> There is no man who hath power over the spirit to retain the spirit, neither hath he power in the day of death ... (*Laughter*) ... neither hath he power in the day of death ... (*Laughter*) ... neither hath he power in the day of death ...' (*III* 194)

References to 'typically Weskerian affirmation' (John Barber) and the 'celebratory conclusion' (Michael Billington) confirm the very positive effect of this production, and justify the subheading on the programme 'A Comedy', which Wesker had not used before.

The comic element in *The Old Ones* is considerable. Even Manny's initial howl of despair lapses into his illogical cross-talk with Gerda:

> EMANUEL: You know, I must stop sleeping out at nights.
> GERDA: Now he's decided.
> EMANUEL: It's too cold and I'm too old to camp out.
> GERDA: Who says you're too old? (*III* 134)

which is built up further by repetition several scenes later:

> EMANUEL: I should stop camping out at nights.
> GERDA: Stop saying. Do!
> EMANUEL: I'm too old to camp out.
> GERDA: Who says you're too old? (*III* 149)

There are funny stories told at the party; there is comedy of character in Sarah's rejection of Rosa's alcoholic gifts: 'You're a good daughter, not everyone's got good daughters, take them back ... You mean well, I'm very grateful, don't argue with me and take them back' (*III* 174); and Millie's ambiguous vagueness was cited by many as the best comic set piece of the play:

113

Climbs on a chair to reach for a pot on top of a cupboard. Inside are five-pound notes. She counts and throws them on the floor.

MILLIE: Five pounds, ten, fifteen, twenty, twenty-five, thirty, thirty-five ... (*Counts on in mumbles, scattering the notes like seeds.*) Seventy-five, eighty, eighty-five, ninety. (*Stops. Looks. Long pause. Descends. Moves to pour tea. Adds milk. Looks back to money on floor.*) It's good to have money. (*III* 148)

The problem with this particular play is that, given the formal debate between pessimism and optimism that runs through it, the atmosphere of humour tends to weight the argument in favour of optimism from the start. One might *expect* a comedy to come down on the side of optimism – so is there any point in pretending to debate the matter at all? In fact Wesker's next comedy, *The Wedding Feast*, does *not* come down on the side of its protagonist's optimism – its corrective comedy is directed against him. But this is not so in *The Old Ones*: the humour is benevolent and takes the edge off the old ones' ills.

Reinforcing this is the character of Sarah. Sarah lives the beneficence that Manny's quotations are trying to prove. Just as, in a Weskerian double monologue that lasts a whole scene, she talks across Boomy's diatribe on Gerda's injuries, planning her own party, so Sarah overwhelms doubts and problems wherever they appear: she refutes Teressa's gibe against 'your working class' with a vigorous argument, reminiscent of the other Sarah's 'electric light' speech, ending 'Everywhere you look – new buildings, new roads, new cities – who puts them there? so leave me alone about my working class' (*III* 160). She consoles her daughter Rosa who is in despair about her total lack of success as a schools careers adviser: 'You'll try again ... With another lot, you'll learn ... Who knows about things in the beginning –' (*III* 172). And she does not condemn Jack for having beaten his wife and driven out his children, but tells of her own pecadillos in scoring off a superior son-in-law. Unlike Manny, she has the whole play behind her – Teressa *does* in fact support Sarah's 'working class' for we are told 'half her pension she sends to left-wing charities' (*III* 160); Rosa *does* try again, and succeeds in getting through to the hostile schoolchildren at last; and Jack stops self-dramatizing for long enough to form an apparently helpful friendship with Millie.

All this tends to overshadow the intrusions of pain and evil into the play – Gerda's being beaten up, Martin's arrest. Almost in self-parody, Sarah says of Gerda 'I'm glad it happened. She'll be more careful next time' (*III* 167) but Gerda is less philosophical. During the last scene, she is lying bandaged on the sofa, but unobtrusive, and Martin of course is not there, so Boomy's speech has to stand for all the irrefutable elements of evil in the pessimism debate. It is not important in itself that we don't know what will happen to Martin, but he should perhaps be more strongly felt than as a significant absence in the festive scene: he should be there with Gerda and Boomy, bearing witness.

So possibly Wesker's vision of a tense, triangular ending would not have been enough to counterpoise the warm, positive tone of the rest of the play – and the original idea had after all been to celebrate the 'survivors'. But there is very little of what Irving Wardle called the 'tom-toms of Weskerian doctrine' beating an explicit message of hope. In fact Wardle's example – Rudi's 'creativity', as seen in his evening-class paintings – is not meant to exemplify everyman's creative potential; on the contrary, their awfulness (*'we receive the first shock of his "work"'* (*III* 144) says the stage direction) indicts his wasted life – paintings this year, singing last year, engineering the year before. Wesker pointed out 'that Rudi *cannot* educate himself, that his paintings are pathetic, and that his butterfly mind skims annually from subject to subject: all of which is observed by his uncle Boomy who says the boy is a dabbler' (P & P November 1972).

Rosa's final breakthrough speech to her schoolchildren, however, is less convincing, and several critics, like Wardle, objected to Susan Engel's 'upraised arm and stirring exhortations about the challenge of literacy'. She is right to warn them that 'It's a big world in which control rests with other people, not *you*. Not you' (*III* 178), and right too to urge them to defend themselves against this state of things, which they can only do by inquiry into it, and by informing themselves: but the shorthand she uses for this – 'Here is a book. Books! Take them. Use them' (*III* 178) – is unrealistic when addressed to the 'poor, used nothings' she has described. How many of them, statistically, *do* read, how many *can* read? Some might have been provoked to ask questions, to find out about their situation, but surely none will be inspired to rush into an (unspecified) reading programme to acquire (unspecified) 'knowledge'. Replying to this objection some years ago in a letter, Wesker simply said: 'but I believe it to be true'. Rosa too seems to be trying to convince by the very strength of her conviction, hence the upraised arm. In the text Wesker directs that Rosa must conclude '*softly, without hope*' (III 179), and the more hopelessly she offers her advice, the more convincing it becomes. But this indicates once more the problem of a play that depends on atmosphere rather than narrative – the balance of the atmosphere can be so easily and so radically altered by production decisions, acting styles, the addition or subtraction of a stage direction. Even the nature of the structure can be in doubt; for instance, some critics took the climax of the play to be Sarah's final party with as Irving Wardle put it, 'the building and decoration of a *succah* (a kind of harvest festival arbour)'. In fact the succah-building, far from being planned as a basis for other action, was itself added afterwards, as Wesker explained:

> John [Dexter] made a physical contribution to *The Old Ones*. The original script was a simple juxtapositioning of these scenes, one alongside the other, ending in a Friday night supper. And John said 'I know what you're trying to do by setting up poetic juxtapositions and not having a plot or a narrative. But what it does need – no matter how delicate – is a framework within which to contain the whole piece. Is it possible to start the preparation of the Friday night supper right from the beginning of the play?' I said 'No, but you could prepare for a Jewish festival', and I suddenly thought of Succoth, because that had building little huts on stage and I knew John liked that sort of [thing]. (Interview with Ronald Hayman in *The Times*, 5 August 1972)

Wesker added rather doubtfully that this 'has given a dimension to the play which I hadn't intended. Because it's highlighted the situation of the Jews in the Diaspora. And the play isn't about that' (though Dexter rejoined that *he* thought it was). Orthodox or not, the *succah* is a positive element and allies with the humour and benevolence to enhance Manny's triumphant flight into confidence at the end. In sum, the effects of this *kind* of comedy overwhelmed Wesker's attempts to leaven the mood with doubts; his next comedy – after writing *The Journalists* – finds him taking a different approach and, within a satirical corrective framework, gaining more secure control of his material.

13

The Wedding Feast

I stopped the cast in the middle of rehearsals one day and said, 'I've got a review for you'. Here it is: 'Possibly because he was aided with a well-constructed story on which *The Wedding Feast* is based, by an infinitely superior writer, Dostoevsky, Arnold Wesker has written his most important play since *Roots,* nearly twenty years ago. Yes, twenty. Gone are the literary pretensions of *The Four Seasons*, the megalomaniac conceptions of *Their Very Own and Golden City*, the heavy philosophical recriminations of *The Friends*, the fey and folksy contemplations of age in *The Old Ones*. Here, at last, Wesker has returned to what he knows best how to handle – simple Norfolk folk in a simple Norfolk setting, playing out the theme of worker-employer relationships'. (TQ 28 p. 10)

Quite right: Wesker was to say 'I'm very grateful to have had for *The Wedding Feast* the best set of reviews since *Chips With Everything*' (TQ 28 p. 10). And a number of them did echo his do-it-yourself crit., both in the nature of the praise and in the use of this play as a stick to beat its predecessors with. Irving Wardle, particularly, liked the second act which 'brings a gain in focus, especially as Wesker has returned to his Norfolk background, which he treats with no less comic sympathy than he did in *Roots*' and Benedict Nightingale agreed that 'in all essentials of content, thought and feeling Dostoevsky has been successfully transformed into Wesker, and not the mushy, woozy Wesker of *The Friends* and *The Old Ones*, but a wide-awake Wesker whose existence we'd all but forgotten'. However much of the praise was less invidious. Nightingale also found 'mental rigour, wit, humour, contemporary point, dramatic tension, the power to seize the attention and not let go until its will is done'. And John Barber called it 'the work of a master of fruity character', though Wesker gloomily detected 'an element in the reviews of, "It's about time we were nice to Arnold"'.

One reason for its accessibility may well be the explicitness of the play's 'message': *The Wedding Feast* is about Louis Litvanov, a self-made, paternalistic, rich Jewish businessman, owner of a

Norfolk shoe factory, who not only believes in equality and fraternity and sympathizes with the intransigence of his work force, but also believes that his sympathy entitles him to loyalty, even love, from them. This delusion, and the vagueness of his beliefs, are comically demolished in the course of the play, and a harsher recognition of class antagonism substituted. First seen at his own birthday party, where he insists on his employees' appreciation, he is asked by his guest Hammond

> supposing you went to their homes. There. Where they live. What then? Would your sense of equality stand up there do you think? Between four dreary working-class walls? Stand up? Would it? (IV 129)

The rest of the action shows just this situation, in which his sense of equality and Louis himself fall flat on their faces over and over again.

By pure chance Louis happens to be passing the house where one of his employees, Knocker White, is celebrating his wedding, and he decides that his boss–employee relationship makes it permissible, indeed desirable, for him to drop in: 'men facing men in a human situation ... Two sides! They'll see two sides of me. And when they're old they'll tell their children and I'll be spoken of with affection, honoured, remembered' (IV 168). The next two acts fulfil Louis's belated foreboding 'that he's about to embark upon one of the most mortifying episodes in his life' (IV 138), as a trail of embarrassments and catastrophes unwinds. Disconcerted by falling into the blancmange on the way in, Louis mangles his prepared speech into an anxious gabble. No one welcomes him, strained silence greets his efforts at bonhomie, he drinks too much too quickly, fails to understand jokes and allusions, and climactically finds himself victim of 'the shoe game', a kind of blind man's buff with flagellation. At the moment of realization that the 'game' has become a hostile demonstration against himself, he tears off the blindfold, and, mercifully, passes out. A last glimpse of him the following dawn shows 'the wreck of Louis' shambling out with clenched teeth and hardened face, surveying the debris of the front-room battleground, and shuffling off with the disillusioned 'Yes, that's the way it has to be' (IV 180).

As Wesker says, it's a comedy, classic in its exposure of social and psychological foibles, and ironic in its satiric twist. There is a fair amount of broad slapstick – Louis falls into the blancmange

118

Above: Their Very Own and Golden City, Wesker's own production, Aarhus, 1973. *Below: The Four Seasons*, Stockholm, 1976.

Above: Wesker (centre) with the cast of *The Friends* in Wales, 1970. *Below: The Journalists*, Wilhelmshaven, 1981.

twice; Stephen, the drunken local reporter, is forcibly carried out and sprays the guests with a soda syphon in the process; the newly-weds' temporary marital couch collapses under them; and there is the running joke of Knocker White, the Yepikhodov character (several critics thought this play 'Chekhovian') and his disaster-prone activities. But many of the characters are not only funny in themselves and not only do their own individual 'turns' – such as the sexy Maureen 'Skirts' Dawson who exposes ever more length of leg, or the offended bride's mother, or the droning compulsive talker Aunt Emily – but innocently or otherwise contribute to the central plot, as each comic figure slips a banana-skin under Louis's dignity. He is not one of the crowd, and he is 'undermined' by every reference he misses, every tone of voice he cannot quite correctly gauge.

Louis learns his lesson, but the ironic twist of the ending is turned on the audience: should we really feel amused and satisfied to see a man deprived of his belief in certain good qualities, even if it is a self-satisfied, naive belief? Not that the goodness of the wedding guests is denied, nor indeed Louis's goodness – it is the delusion that goodness on both sides in itself justifies this economic relationship, or any other economic relationship. Hammond asks 'are all Jewish businessmen as paternalistic as you?' and Louis objects 'That's what you call it? Give everything a name and dismiss it' (*IV* 128). He is not a fool – he hasn't risen from poverty to capitalism by being a fool – but the accusation is true. Louis *is* paternalistic, in that he thinks that kindness, 'good wages and a pleasant atmosphere' (*IV* 128) sanctify the status quo. He has to lose his wilful blindness in the face of inequalities. The final 'despair of his position', once the message has been put across to him and to us, was challenged by Tony Coult in *Plays and Players*: 'Now no socialist would accept that, and I assume Wesker wouldn't either'. No socialist would deny the existence of class divisions in practice: Louis had been doing his best to paper over the cracks with paternalism, and his 'the way it has to be' betokens an acceptance of his own role, given the facts. This is spelt out for us by Kate, his Marxist secretary and Knocker's sister, speaking to the unconscious Louis:

Just give them the rate for their work and the sweet, sweet *illusion* that they're equal to any man. Stop pretending it's a reality. (*Pause.*) And don't be kind or ashamed or apologetic for your money. You go around behaving like that, how shall we be able to hit you when the time comes, bor? (*IV* 178-9)

Neither Louis nor Wesker is saying that things *cannot* be any different – simply that harsh reality must be faced until the 'time comes' for change.

The theme gains depth from Louis's evident attractiveness to audiences. 'The first-night audience appeared sympathetic towards the character of Litvanov, who stood naked and honest before them' reported Dick Wilcocks in the *Times Educational Supplement*, and the *Daily Express* critic added 'We can all identify with Litvanov', while Rosemary Say even feared that the sympathy for him was 'unwarranted'. David Swift as Louis in the Leeds production was highly praised, 'played as well as it is written,' said B. A. Young 'a little bald-pated man, now ingratiating, now bullying, but determined to impose his ingratiation by bullying if necessary; then at the Birmingham Rep. production the following year David Suchet, who 'dominates the stage with squat vigour and a powerful, rasping voice' (*Times Literary Supplement*) was equally triumphant. Without the sympathy for Louis and for his after all very natural wish to understand and get on with his employees, the play would be a good deal simpler – just a 'clobber the boss' cartoon. The puncturing of Louis's delusions is the more effective if the audience identifies with his wish to be loved. So he has his whims and anxieties; he gets carried away by his enthusiasm and then feels guilty, as when his exclamatory speeches are followed by Kate's remonstration 'you're shouting' and his subsiding with 'I'm Jewish, I shout' (*IV* 122), or, later, 'I'm in good spirits, I shout' (*IV* 133). Not a fool, he doesn't need Kate to tell him that he tries too hard – alone in his bathroom he ends a soliloquy '(*Mimicking, shouting.*) Louis, you're shouting. (*Takes off pants, finds himself confronting another mirror – naked and vulnerable. Softly, sadly.*) I'm human, I shout!' (*IV* 131), But usually his comic traits are linked more directly with his main comic flaw – his ostrich-like ignoring of his boss-role. He see-saws between being overbearing and egalitarian. For instance, his patronage of his operative Bonky Harris's paintings:

LOUIS: You paint don't you?
BONKY: My hobby is my –

LOUIS: And I want to see them.
BONKY: I don't show –
LOUIS: I mean, *may* I see them? Please?
BONKY: I don't show no one what I do.
LOUIS: I want to buy some.
BONKY: I don't sell –
LOUIS: I mean I'd *like* to buy some. Please. (*IV* 133)

Robert Cushman, however, was one of the few who thought that 'Louis himself strains belief, and his secretary annihilated it', partly because of the expository prologue. Kate, the secretary, has a smaller role than her not dissimilar namesake in *Golden City*, but it is probably more successful. She is a bright grammar-school lass who has acquired Marxism and cynicism in growing older, but it is her interaction with the exasperating Louis and with her (if anything) even more exasperating family – and their unimpressed comments about her – that round her character out.

The source of most reservations about the play was the 'prologue', in which local journalist Stephen Bullock functions as a narrator commenting on Louis's background and character, supplemented by illustrations from Kate and Louis's manager, David. The explanation starts with a straight anecdote told by Louis about his father, then goes on to examples of Louis quixotic paternalism from Kate and David in turn, but with Stephen adding dramatized dialogue. Then Stephen virtually plays out a two-handed sketch with Louis. B. A. Young summarized the objections of most critics to this prologue:

This is both composed and directed in a manner quite unlike the rest of the play; stylized writing involves a tiresome narrator (whom Brett Usher makes as little tiresome as he can) and a good deal of soliloquy. Besides telling us what we need to be told about Litvanov, it tells us much more than we need to know and have little interest in. It also gives Mr Wesker his opportunity to indulge in politics.

More succinctly, Robert Cushman called it a 'disaster area'. Wesker himself was defiant about his structuring: 'I think it works. I think the first act works marvellously. I just don't understand what the critics are talking about when they complain about a confusion of styles' (TQ 28 p. 17). He was all in favour of mixing styles: 'It would be intrusive only if the mood or the texture or the language was different, but in *The Wedding Feast* it isn't' (TQ 28 p. 18). But some people did object to Stephen's tone. The irony is laid on quite heavily – 'Poor Louis Litvanov, husband, father, idealist ...' (*IV* 132) – and is irritating at times, more irritating perhaps than Stephen is intended to be, although the guests too seem to get irritated with Stephen during the reception. The problem may be that one is never sure how much bias to allow for when he is acting as narrator.

Robert Cushman also surmised that the prologue 'may well have scared managements off'. This is what actually happened, as Wesker recalled: 'In retrospect, I began to wonder whether I was all wrong, when people were turning down the play because they claimed that the first act was so different from the other two', but he felt it had the advantage that it 'eliminated all that awful plot-making that so often prevents the process of the play from unfolding'. Hopefully, 'those first scenes set out the personality of Litvanov in such a way that you're dying to know what happens to him in that situation' (TQ 28, p. 18). What ultimately happens may come as a surprise, in spite of the forebodings of disaster: Gerard Dempsey called it 'an uneasy play' because 'for two-thirds of its length we are lulled along on a warm tide of recognizable humour. Then, in the last act, Wesker pounces' – the humiliations are comic until the crucial demolition of Louis in the course of the shoe game. As in Pinter's *The Birthday Party*, Louis becomes the victim, beaten by a circle of shoe-wielding players. As Tony Coult described it, 'it is a moment of chilling power, a shocking little metaphor which shows the bitter seed that remains at the heart of all management/worker relations no matter how much good-will and care are expended to sweeten it'. And Robert Cushman called this ritual 'the most, successful, believable and suggestive in any of Mr. Wesker's plays'. Benedict Nightingale regretted that 'this climactic humiliation lacks savagery', but Wesker had been concerned to keep the episode naturalistic and untainted by comedy of menace:

> They become intoxicated. The beating grows. It's no longer a game. A mob mentality takes over, and each tap becomes more malevolent, the sound of the whack more frequent, until all control is lost and they simply crowd in and beat him about the body (not the face.) (*IV* 176)

It is a psychological and social phenomenon, but not abnormal or mystic or psychotically sadistic. And of course the blindfold neatly completes the metaphor by symbolizing Louis's blindness to reality. It is after the shoe game that Kate, who has been out, returns to pick up the pieces, and tells Louis that equality between employee and boss is an 'illusion'. The 'reality' of power sharing is something Louis is never going to bring himself to concede. 'I suppose I do identify with Litvanov: he's not me but I do identify with him' (TQ 28 p. 18), said Wesker wryly, because a lot of the 'paternalist' criticism levelled at Litvanov had come his way during the Centre Fortytwo period.

14

The Merchant

In Shakespeare's *Merchant of Venice* Shylock is a miserly suspicious Jew, whose hostility to Christians, inflamed when his daughter elopes with a Gentile, breaks all rational bounds and impels him to hold his debtor, the equally hostile and anti-semitic Antonio, to a bond by which he forfeits a pound of his flesh. 'The portrayal of Shylock offends for being a lie about the Jewish character,' Wesker said: 'I seek no pound of flesh but, like Shylock, I'm unforgiving, unforgiving of the play's contribution to the world's astigmatic view and murderous hatred of the Jew.'[1] And Jonathan Miller's 1970 production for the National Theatre, with Laurence Olivier as Shylock, focussed this objection:

> When Portia suddenly gets to the bit about having a pound of flesh but no blood, it flashed on me that the kind of Jew I know would stand up and say 'Thank god!' My first thought was that perhaps one day I would be able to do a production of Shakespeare's *Merchant* in which that's the way it would happen, and I discussed this with Ewan Hooper one day. He said, 'That's very interesting, but you'd have to do a lot of rewriting'. I thought about it, and realised it would be simpler to write a new play. (TQ 28 p. 21)

So, Wesker went on, 'If the "real" Shylock would have thanked god for the get-out Portia gave him, one had to work out how he had got himself involved in a contract which he clearly didn't want'. Working backwards from this, he made Shylock and Antonio friends, close friends, and the bond therefore became a joke between friends, never expected to fall due. But once the bond *does* fall due, it has to be kept, so as not to create a precedent of contract-breaking which next time might be used against the Jews (given that the Venetians are longing for an excuse to break through the protective laws and victimize the hated Jews). The ghetto's view of the bond would be 'No! having bent the law for us, how often will they bend it for themselves and then we'll live in even greater uncertainties than before' (*IV* 243).

Quite a lot of Shakespeare's material was jettisoned – 'I sloughed off more and more of the original as I went along. For example some early notes show how I was going to handle the Lancelot Gobbo scenes, but in the end I dispensed with them entirely' (TQ 28 p. 22). The three main stories however were retained – the bond, the eloping daughter, and Portia's wooing by means of a choice of three caskets. These all undergo something of a sea-change with the new, pro-Shylock point of view. Because Shylock is now a sympathetic character, rather than a tyrant whom any daughter would want to leave, Jessica's elopement has to be re-motivated. It becomes an element in a generation-gap rebellion: Jessica is given her father's own independent character and consequently Shylock's loving assertiveness is shown as intolerable: her elopement is a bid for escape. Then the main love plot retains its outline, turning as it does on the will of Portia's late father bequeathing her to the suitor who choses correctly between three caskets, but the impracticality of this fairy-tale situation is not glossed over but stressed as an example and metaphor of the way patriarchal society has the right to dominate even highly educated and intelligent Renaissance women such as Portia (and indeed Jessica). In both these subplots, the subordinate position of women is also underlined by the unworthiness of their suitors: Jessica's Lorenzo is one of Wesker's rebels-rather-than-revolutionaries – 'I despise power yet so much offends me that I want power to wipe out the offence' (IV 219), he says – and is bigoted as well; while Portia's Bassanio is 'a confidence trickster' (TQ 28 p. 24) and a manipulator.

Wesker was from the first rather unnerved at 'taking on Shakespeare', and wary of being considered a blasphemous paranoid fool, – an anxiety fuelled by John Russell Brown when, discussing the first draft, he emphasized 'how risky it was writing in the shadow of Shakespeare'. And this was to be the shocked attitude of some American reviewers. No British critics took this view, being less overawed by their own bard, and already having the precedent of Edward Bond's *Lear* before them. The validity of the new version was taken for granted – in fact several thought it was a jolly good idea. But in spite of acceptance in principle, it seemed that some aspects of Wesker's play were being judged not on their own merits but by reference to the original. For instance, the changes meant that there was no snarling confrontation at the end, and some critics missed this: Rosemary Say couldn't see where the dramatic conflict lay, if Shylock and Antonio were friends. But Shylock's choice between the life of his friend and the safety of his community is the classic –or neo-classic – love-duty conflict, and a very powerful one. It is just a different *kind* of dramatic conflict from the racial antagonism of the earlier play. Victoria Radin in the *Observer* thought that the play 'desperately needs a villain other than the loutish young aristocrats Wesker makes such fun of'. Why? Because Shakespeare's play had one. Being a twentieth-century playwright Wesker was interested less in the overweening individual villain or hero *per se* than in social pressures acting on the individual – as Ned Chaillet said, the play has 'debts to history and social structures that Shakespeare never found'.

Shylock himself is a familiar Wesker character – he has all the enthusiasm, extroversion and verbosity of Manny from *The Old Ones* and Louis from *The Wedding Feast*, but he is not finally a comic character, and in the embittered and melancholy side of his nature there are echoes of Manfred in *The Friends* and Boomy in *The Old Ones*. As with Manny and Louis, Shylock's eagerness and volatility hurl him painfully against the sharp corners of life – his sister Rivka's speech to him is the key to his character:

> Oh Shylock, my young brother, I've watched you, wandering away from Jewish circles, putting your nose out in alien places. I've watched you be restless and pretend you can walk in anybody's streets. Don't think I've not understood you; suffocating in this little yard, waiting for your very own scholar to arrive. It made me ache to watch you, looking for moral problems to sharpen your mind, for disputations – as if there weren't enough troubles inside these peeling walls. But you *can't* pretend you're educated, just as you can't pretend you're not an alien or that this Ghetto has no walls ... Pretend, pretend, pretend! All your life! Wanting to be what you're not. Imagining the world as you want. (*IV* 242)

Hemmed in by laws about what Jews may and may not do, he has less choice in his exploits than Louis, but he still shares Louis's illusions; and like him, but more savagely, Shylock is brought down by the social realities of his time. Also like Louis, he is vain, reminding Antonio of his reputation as benefactor to the refugees in the Ghetto: 'They talk, you see, Antonio! I'm a name in in my community. From nobody to somebody, a name!' (*IV* 205). It is his enthusiasm that appeals to Antonio: who is grateful to have

126

got 'caught up in your – your passion, your hoardings, your – your vices' (*IV* 194). David Swift, who played Shylock at Birmingham, had also played Louis in the Leeds production of *The Wedding Feast*, but didn't achieve the same mixture of bounce and vitality – perhaps purposely. (John Barber described his Shylock as 'a worthy owl', which doesn't seem to capture the overbearing and proud side of his character.)

His family find him overwhelming. 'But he bullies with it all' complains Jessica. Yet his generosity is genuine, and this rather than vanity underlies his prompt offer of the interest-free loan of three thousand ducats to Antonio (for the obnoxious Bassanio). It is Antonio who insists that there *must* be a legal bond. Precisely because the Jews are only grudgingly protected by the laws of Venice, the laws are all that stand between them and mob hatred. So the joke about the pound of flesh is Shylock's last sulky kick against the mean position society forces him to take towards his friend.

Not, then, being an overweening villain, Shylock's position at the end of the play is necessarily different from his predecessor's, and again Victoria Radin thought this to Wesker's disadvantage – his Shylock lacked 'tragic dignity'. But there *is* a dignity, though not the same kind of dignity as in Shakespeare. Wesker's Shylock does not have the famous 'Hath not a Jew eyes?' speech. For Wesker, the speech 'was so powerful that it dignified the anti-semitism. An audience, it seemed to me, could come away with its prejudices about the Jew confirmed but held with an easy conscience because they thought they'd heard a noble plea for extenuating circumstances'[1] and elsewhere he commented 'That seemed to me hollow – after the holocaust, just hollow'. Not only was the Shakespearean Jew innately wicked, but his claims to equal humanity meant that he was fully responsible for his inhumanity. In Wesker's play the well-known lines are actually given to Lorenzo, who is acting as a kind of prosecuting counsel and incidentally furthering a certain political line of his own, trying to establish a mild, rational persona for himself. The speech is moreover broken up by outraged protests from Shylock – cries of 'No, no, NO!' and the challenge that 'If I am unexceptionally like any other man, then I need no exceptional portraiture' (*IV* 259). To Wesker, the patronizing tone of the speech was reminiscent of 'the Catholic decision to forgive the Jews' (TQ 28 p. 24), and David Nathan found in Shylock's protests 'the same ring of impatience that boils up when others graciously acknowledge "Israel's right to exist"'. It is a part of Shylock's pride that his reaction here is sheer impatience, not dignity.

Nonetheless, Wesker's Shylock accumulates a dignity that is no less than in Shakespeare's play. Defeated but not submissive to the forces he had rashly invoked, he asks Antonio to keep a dignified silence in court. He doesn't want explanations of his defence of his community, as if he were claiming to be a hero – 'It would be grotesque' (*IV* 247). This pride is linked, as he admits, with a contempt for men who have acquiesced in a society which allows this kind of situation to arise.

> I am sometimes horrified by the passion of my contempt for men. Can I be so without pity for their stupidities, compassion for their frailties, excuses for their cruelties? It is as though these books of mine have spoken too much, too long; the massacres by kings, the deathly little spites of serfs, the oppressive jealousies and hurts of scholars, who had more learning than wisdom. Too much, Antonio, too much. Seeing what men have done, I know with great weariness the pattern of what they will do, and I have such contempt, such contempt it bewilders me. (*IV* 247)

Manfred's contempt for the 'Englishman', is echoed here, and Shylock goes on to unite Manny's and Boomy's perspectives on mankind, finding the pessimistic view overshadowing the other:

> The balance, dear friend, the balance! We can't always cheat the scales of history. Take those books, one by one, place on one side thoses which record man's terrible deeds, and on the other their magnificence. Do it! Deed for deed! Healing beside slaughter, building beside destruction, truth beside lie. Do it! Do it! (*Pause*.) My contempt, sometimes, knows no bounds. And it has destroyed us. (*IV* 248)

Then after Portia's nullification of the bond has been followed by the confiscation of all his property, including his books, his final speech shows him as embittered as in Shakespeare's play, and more dignified in his exit from the court:

> No. Take my books. The law must be observed. We have need of the law, what need do we have of books? Distressing, disturbing things, besides. Why, dear friend, they'd even make us question laws. Ha! And who in his right mind would want to do that? Certainly not old Shylock. Take my books. Take everything. I do not want the law departed from, not one letter departed from.

(*Sound of song.*)
Perhaps now is the time to make that journey to Jerusalem. Join those other old men on the quayside, waiting to make a pilgrimage, to be buried there – ach! What do I care! My heart will not follow me, wherever it is. My appetites are dying, dear friend, for anything in this world. I am so tired of men. (*IV 263–4*)

This is his only comment on his victimization – present and past.

The court scene, the elopement and Bassanio's choice of casket all come in the second half, with the result that, for some critics, the first act seemed not to have enough action. In his diary while writing the opening section Wesker went back over what happened in Shakespeare's opening: 'In the very first scene Bassanio asks for the loan, in the second Portia reveals her obligation to the caskets, by the third the bond is made with Shylock. I'd reached scene 3 and the only part of the plot revealed was to do with Portia and the caskets'. The main criticism of the play was that there was too much historical explanation – a 'massive teach-in on historical and literary attitudes to the Jews', Sheridan Morley called it, and Sally Aires in *Plays and Players* noted that most of this came in Act One. One potential problem is the big set piece expositions, such as the account of how knowledge survived the dark ages to blossom into the Renaissance, given by Shylock at Antonio's dinner table. But this, like Manfred's physics speech, is written as a special turn to be *performed*, not just delivered. The stage direction says: 'Then Shylock tells his story with mounting excitement and theatricality, using whatever is around him for props, moving furniture, food, perhaps even people, like men on his chessboard of history'. John Dexter in the American production began by getting Zero Mostel to move tables about, then later changed to moving people, as Wesker recorded in his diary:

John re-blocks Renaissance speech using Graziano and Bassanio. Great laughter among cast when Shylock names the city-states as 'Milan, Genoa, Venice, and –' taking Bassanio by the hand and sitting him down; '– Florence!' Then later Zero can't resist saying:
'And where were the books, Florence?' Everyone convulsed ... Meanwhile the Renaissance speech seems funnier and lighter. In using the men it also becomes a story to which people on stage are listening and so the audience will listen. Antonio becomes Cassiodorus. Lovely. The books are a bowl of fruit! And the printing press is a chair which he tosses over to Lorenzo. Then he throws the fruit – representing the

books – at Bassanio and Graziano. The 'little lost spring' becomes the last apple which, when the Ghetto bells ring to call his back, he eats.

A more palpable problem is the warehouse scene, Act One scene five, where Lorenzo, Bassanio and Graziano have a long discussion about power and privilege, aristocracy and economics in Venice. Though Wesker said that the play was about his usual preoccupations, one of which was the nature of power, this discussion – with its references to Savonarola and Venetian history – seems to be at too many removes from Shylock's central predicament, and lacks direction, in spite of the power and riches being visually illustrated by the wares. Wesker's diary: 'John blocks the warehouse scene and it's a joy to watch him delightedly develop his idea to have Graziano unfold bales of cloth to dress Bassanio, ending himself being tied up in many colours'. Trade is already established as important, but it hardly seems relevant to know whether the Venetian nobility began as fishermen or as something else, or about the difference between 'long' and 'short' noble families.

Wesker had begun by researching into the period and the history of the Jews in Venice especially – their situation there was a particularly appropriate example of their situation everywhere, as it was in Venice that the word 'ghetto' first originated: it was an abandoned iron-founding district (from 'gettare', to cast iron) where the Jews were relegated. American summer-school students at Boulder, Colorado, had helped with preliminary reading of secondary sources, then Wesker had become absorbed in further reading over a considerable period. When he began writing, he felt that 'much of it is work already written in notes, I'm just creating the place for them to sit in'. There is nothing more painful for a writer in this position, postively overloaded with fascinating detail, than to have to leave the bulk of it out, and though this is eventually what had to happen, some material like the 'long' and 'short' families must have been included for its intrinsic interest rather than for its relevance to Shylock.

This was one of the reasons why the National Theatre did not care for the play. Director Peter Hall wrote to Wesker's agent that it was 'as if Arnold were really so fond of his subject that he couldn't bear to leave out anything that occurred to him'. Another objection was to what one could call the fullness of the dialogue:

the National felt that the characters 'expressed too much, that every character was articulate and expressive of every single point of view that Wesker might take about every aspect of the situation'. But this does not take account of the fact that the context and characters in *The Merchant* are *not* naturalistic. In performance, it was the amount of discussion, not its explicitness, that weighed on critics.

The National Theatre having declined the play, the British premiere eventually took place at Birmingham Repertory Theatre. The reviews were almost as good as those for *The Wedding Feast* – the three major Sunday papers on the whole disliked it, with some qualifications, but the *Times*, *Guardian*, *Financial Times* and *Morning Star* were using terms like 'double and totally unexpected triumph', 'a compelling play', a 'mighty work'. The most hostile review was Bernard Levin's in the *Sunday Times*, who found it 'grimly literary'. Obviously the texture and style of the language had been a major hurdle for Wesker – but it didn't seem to worry audiences that he was not imitating Shakespearean verse. As he said, 'I'd have been mad to go into competition with Shakespeare as a poet!' Nor is the play entirely composed of long speeches – before Shylock's 'contempt' speech there is an interchange between Antonio and Shylock, elliptical, and with extensive unspoken implications left to the subtext. Antonio begins: 'I cannot raise the money now', to which Shylock replies 'I know'. They then rehearse the constraints of their situation:

SHYLOCK: I must not set a precedent.
ANTONIO: I know.
SHYLOCK: *You* said. *You* taught.
ANTONIO: Shylock, Shylock, I'm not afraid.
SHYLOCK: Oh friend! What have I done to you?
   (*Pause.*)
ANTONIO: Your yellow hat belongs to both of us. I'm party to the
   mockery as well.
SHYLOCK: I know.
ANTONIO: An act of schoolboy defiance when such times should be
   taken seriously. We shall both be put to death.
SHYLOCK: I know.
ANTONIO: I by you. You by them.
SHYLOCK: I know, I know.
ANTONIO: We know, we know. We keep saying we know so much.
   (*IV 246–7*)

In a way Wesker had found an ideal context for his linguistic development, and one which had already been explored by his contemporary, John Arden, who had noted how a historical setting made verse dialogue immediately acceptable: 'in a modern play one is conscious all the time that this is not the way these people would really be speaking in this situation, whereas no one can really know how men *talked* to each other in the past'. And the same is true of other, more formal speech styles. Costume and setting at once distance the characters from the audience and create different expectations. So, Shylock can lament over Jessica's elopement in articulate phrases – 'What wretched, alien philosophy has taken up your mind, muddied it with strange fervours?' (a line Levin particularly disliked) – without having to water it down to fit a twentieth-century drawing room.

The very first production of *The Merchant* took place in Aarhus, Denmark, and there was an anxious period during which various managements looked askance at the play, until Eddie Kulukundis, who had backed *The Friends* in 1970, expressed interest and sent the script on to John Dexter, with, as Wesker recalls in his diary, enthusiastic results:

> Have just been to the National. It was while talking to Peter Hall that I turned and saw a beaming John Dexter. He opened his arms and we embraced. Damn him, he's irresistible for me I suppose. Surely I've said this before but he's a first love. He directed my first five plays, and they were his first five. Within seconds he was saying: 'I've read *The Merchant* and isn't it good. It's very good indeed'

The first English language production was set up for New York, after an out-of-town run. Prospects were promising: as Wesker put it, 'Zero Mostel was booked to open my play *The Merchant* on Broadway – a two million dollar advance was expected and people regarded me as though I'd inherited a bank'. He had some misgivings about Zero Mostel's performance in the early rehearsals, because although 'His powers of concentration are tremendous, he's a great professional', his 'over-acting' was worrying: 'I can't understand how he doesn't know to start explosive speeches at the bottom in order to give himself somewhere to go'. Zero theorized about 'believing one should hold back until the stage', on which Wesker commented 'It was nonsense because he's been yelling and screaming through rehearsals and already had smashed two glasses – so what was he holding back?' John Dexter wanted to reserve any strong criticism until after the play had had its first preview at Philadelphia, and the cuts in the text and problems with the set too had to be settled at Philadelphia so that 'at Philadelphia' began to sound like 'at Philippi', and for Zero Mostel it was indeed to be Philippi. He completed one performance then was taken to hospital with a 'virus infection' just before the second night. A week later he died of an aneurism. Naturally everyone in the company was shattered, and there were feelings of guilt too – Wesker felt 'My play had killed him. He dieted for it, and was under pressure for it and – silly bugger! He overdid it. Oh Zero, Zero, Zero!' and again, later, recollecting how he had complained of Zero's slovenly, badly articulated dialogue, he noted 'I've heard that one of the symptoms of Zero's ailment, aneurism, is a slurring of the speech. How terrible knowing that'.

Wesker kept a full diary of the production, (as everyone knew at the time: at one point he records 'John glanced at the notes I was taking – like Johnson making sure Boswell got it right – and added CENSORED!') It is clear from this diary that with Zero Mostel's death the atmosphere of the long rehearsal period began to deteriorate. To begin with Wesker's presence at and participation in rehearsals had been welcomed. Jocelyn Herbert was designing the sets as she had for Wesker's early plays, so there had been a sense of the old team being back together again. The only major disagreement was about the credibility of Shylock's position when the bond is demanded of him – would he have the nerve to cut out Antonio's heart, and, if he did, would the law protect the Ghetto from reprisals? This point was raised by John Clements who was playing Antonio, and made a convincing case for Shylock's having a sympathetic change of heart. This Wesker resisted, as being too sentimental. John Dexter asked if Wesker would be able to bring himself to kill him (Dexter): at first he replied that he would, and then retracted. It was a difficult challenge to answer, and Wesker ended by admitting the insolubility of the dilemma, but stressing its irrelevance to his theme:

> You're talking about another kind of play. My play is about 'barbaric laws – barbaric bonds', simply that. That's all I want to explore. There's a beautiful friendship, everything seems cosy, along comes a godson to borrow money, no real problem there – but it's the seed of the beginning, because then the reality has to be faced – the laws of

Venice, barbaric laws which produced barbaric actions, even though innocently conceived. Now, you want a play about what happens when a man actually has to kill his friend. What does he do? I didn't think about it this way when I was writing but I now see that I instinctively avoided what I felt I couldn't honestly handle. I don't know what Shylock would do – nor what I would do – and so I didn't let the situation get that far. I use Shakespeare's device and bring on Portia. Fault me for that but that's the play I wanted to write.

It is interesting that in fact *only* David Nathan of the *Jewish Chronicle* picked up the pragmatic 'reprisals' point:

> If there is a flaw in the logic of the play it is that Wesker does not explore the possibility of what would happen to the Ghetto Jews if Shylock had been allowed to use the knife. Would the Venetian mob have the same respect for the law as the Venetian patricians? Or rather would they have rampaged through the Ghetto as they have done throughout history even on the merest suspicion of Jewish involvement in a Christian death?

In a letter to Nathan, Wesker admitted to being still not satisfied with the dilemma, but, as with 'Shakespeare's device', in practice it was something that audiences accepted.

But after Philadephia, difficulties seemed to snowball. The advantage to Wesker of participating in rehearsals so that his final vision of the play could be tested against its actual performance carried the corresponding disadvantage that an author on the spot could be pressured to make alterations and cuts convenient to the company but perhaps not in the best interests of the play. The production company demanded half an hour of cuts, and John Dexter was their intermediary in finding them: he had begun by echoing Wesker's fascination with Venetian history, but now he changed his mind – 'the worst excesses, indulgences in historic detail, under the view that "they" should know what "we" know, I encouraged you in and fed you more of'. The anxiety and conflict soured the atmosphere still further. For instance Wesker recalled the suspicion and hostility at the end of *The Old Ones* and saw a similar hostility growing up here:

> I arrive at the theatre. There seems to be a relationship between John, Andy Philips (lighting designer) and Jocelyn. I feel it's a relationship of the English, the Gentiles, the interpreters. John's bought two bottles of wine, Jocelyn has bought some Camembert and rusks. I hear John say

'we're going to have a party for the next three days'. But there's no greeting to me, no 'come on, Arnold, wine to see us through these days!' I decide to go upstairs and watch from the balcony where Susan from publicity and a photographer are sitting.

But later Dexter gave Wesker his version of the incident:

> Something John told me was an indication of the problems of our difference in personalities. I was staggered. He said how upset he'd been, how anxious, that, the other afternoon in the theatre when we were approaching the first preview, I'd gone up to the balcony. He'd thought 'My God, Arnold's gone off to write another *Guardian* article' ... I leapt at John and told him how they'd completely misread the situation and how I too had thought we'd reached another *Old Ones* moment and had written in my journal that it seemed to me like the period when I'd written in the *Guardian*. We'd both felt exactly the same anxieties, but I'd fled from what I thought was their unfriendliness. They'd seen it as me abandoning the team to be photographed! How *could* it have happened?

The question of cuts became obsessional, the frequent changes undermined respect for the text, the court scene was rewritten, with an ensuing near-mutiny of the cast. At the final stage, John Dexter made more cuts while Wesker was in England, and though Dexter was upset that 'I've done something I've never done before which is cut while you weren't here ... it's blazing inside me and it's all a mess and why I did it and I want to get it off my chest', the cuts remained, and further increased Wesker's anxiety:

> What do I feel? A mixture of many things. Some humiliation to be so powerless, to have had it done behind my back before the company. Angry that lines are cut because actors can't do them. Ashamed that a lot of what gave me pleasure in the play is now gone ... I wanted to write an epic, now it's neat, Readers' Digest, and my share is that I can't really stop it – the actors' work, John's work, the producers' money *are* to be considered. And if it is a success I'll be earning a lot of money on something I don't really feel is mine. There's the humiliation. And a feeling of – rape. That's it! *That's* the nature of the humiliation. And some of the shame lies in suspecting myself of wanting to 'take my money and run' in order to pay my income tax, and the solicitors' fees for the RSC law suit.

Because of the cuts and his usual feeling that a play recedes further from its author as it gets nearer to the first night, Wesker was depressed about the opening. Consequently it should hardly have

135

surprised him that several of the New York critics, including the all important, make-or-break *New York Times* reviewer, did not care for the play. Yet he *was* surprised because his impression was that the first night had overwhelmed everyone: 'It was all electric. The audience laughed, applauded in between speeches and – I looked at their faces – were touchingly attentive ... In the interval the buzz was high and everyone was convinced they were in on a triumph, were witnessing an event'. This could have had an element of wishful thinking, perhaps, but a Hollywood columnist discribed the atmosphere of the party afterwards at Sardi's, in the same terms:

> Sardi's was like New Year's Eve after the opening of Arnold Wesker's *The Merchant* at the Plymouth Theatre. The electric excitement of a sure-fire success permeated the room ... As the evening wore on the mood of celebration suddenly changed ... The same critics who have been deploring the epidemic of revivals because there are no new playwrights of any distinction blasted Wesker for tampering with Shakespeare. Tampering, how? Wesker is no cribbing Bacon, but one of the most penetrating creative playwrights in the British and American theatre. For Wesker to be dismissed by a former second-string movie reviewer and a few TV critics is disgraceful.

The *New York Times* reviewer was indeed comparatively new to the job, whereas ironically the incumbent of the previous twenty years, Clive Barnes, was saying on a (less prestigious) radio programme: 'This is Wesker's finest play, the most deeply felt theatrically, the most beautifully written'. The *New York Times* review was so influential that this kind of praise there would have guaranteed a long run. It was a gamble, and it had not come off.

15

Love Letters on Blue Paper

Wesker was eventually to be performed at the National Theatre, first with the stage version of his television play *Love Letters on Blue Paper* in 1978, which he directed himself, then in 1981 with *Caritas*, one of the two plays he wrote after *The Merchant*.

The love letters in question are written by Sonia, an otherwise dour and inarticulate wife to Victor, her husband, who is dying of leukaemia. (She is not supposed to know this, but it is not clear whether she does or not.) Though the characters are very different, ent, there are insistent echoes from *The Friends*, inasmuch as both are much preoccupied with death. Reminded in an interview that 'You realize you'll have to swear off deathbeds for a while?', Wesker agreed 'Yes, I do realize that. I really do realize that' (TQ 28 p. 21). Victor like Esther wants to live, in spite of the social ills that he, as an active Trade Union official, has spent a lifetime fighting against – to little avail: 'Still! Still, still, still! After what we did. All we did! (*Long pause.*) And yet – I don't want to leave any of it. I'd live with it all – just so long as I lived' (*III* 202). And *Love Letters* shares with *The Friends* some of the same origins – the letters of Robert Copping, an old friend of Wesker's:

> One day he came back, dying of leukaemia. I watched him for some days in Guy's Hospital, dying. And his wife Valerie showed me some letters written to a friend of his, a psychiatrist, – one describing how he first was told he had leukaemia, and the other telling how, after the initial shock, he began to think that 'Karl Marx is dead, Freud is dead ...' The letters were very impressive, and touched me. (TQ 28 p. 20)

In beginning *The Friends* Wesker had referred to other parts of the letters, where Copping had said:

> It is of interest that under this test, and without any kind of emotional euphoria, I find it easier to accept the rightness of the universe rather than a doctrine of despair ... (TQ 2 p. 78)

Sonia's letters on blue paper serve like Simone's exhortations – but retrospectively, looking back over their married life, insisting on the value their relationship has had. Victor is an atheist and not only has no belief in a life after death, but is ashamed of impulses to canvass the possibility, believing then to stem from sheer cowardice:

> And then I got angry and I say to myself: 'Darkness! Nothing! When you're dead that's it. Over! Done! If you want satisfaction, Victor lad, then look to your life, your political battles, the fights you fought for other men.' But who can do that for long? Dwell on his past and go scratching for bits of victory? Eh? A smug man perhaps. But I'm not a smug man, Maurice, never was. (*III* 215-16)

These triumphs are no use to him as justification of a whole life; it is Sonia's recollection of their life together, quarrels as well as happiness, that gives real substance and weight to his past. Towards the end, Victor too begins to recall 'In the early days she used to laugh a great deal. At predicaments' (*III* 225), and he goes on to tell an anecdote about Sonia's learning to drive, while she cuts in with reminiscences about their son's babyhood. Mostly she traces what the relationship has meant by its effect on herself – the way Victor has changed her from being 'plain-minded' and 'soft-brained' to being able to express herself and think. Her own personal pleasures, such as gardening, have come from him: '– the cycle of things. *You* used to be like that, loving the cycle of things. It's you I got it from' (*III* 217). And she sums up what she owes him: 'I've been a white sheet, a large white canvas and you've drawn the world upon me, given outline to what was mysterious and frightening in me' (*III* 231).

Victor's acceptance of death comes as he relates his own life to the lives of the past, in the words of Rober Copping's letter:

> I thought: Leonardo Da Vinci is dead. And that seemed reassuring. So I went on: Mozart is dead. Socrates is dead, Shakespeare, Buddha, Jesus, Gandhi, Marx, Keir Hardie – they're all dead. And some day Sonia will die. And my son, Graeme, he'll be dead, and my daughter Hilda, and their son Jake, and so will the grand-children ... And there seemed a great unity to it all. A great simplicity. Comforting. (*III* 232)

This is not of course his way of diminishing these great men, nor of gathering comfort from the thought of his family sharing his doom – it is as he says the sense of unity, just as Esther in *The Friends* felt that she was in a way responsible for, and thus a part of, the centuries of accumulated sensibility. And Sonia's last letter promises him the meaning and survival of death that he has not dared imagine for himself:

> There will be, my darling one, I know it, a blinding light ... There will come this flash, this light of a colour we've never seen before. It's a glorious moment beloved. Even for the simpleton, even for him, his foolishness falls away just as from the madman his madness falls away. In the instant they know death so they know truth. In the blinding light of truth they know death. One and the same. I promise you, trust me, love O my love O my Victor O my heart. (*III* 233–4)

As Wesker said, these are the two halves of the play:

> There's the man who's facing death, who is dying and doesn't know how to cope with it and needs to talk with someone, but doesn't want to upset his wife. On the other hand, there's the wife, who senses that all this is taking place, and instinctively finds the right thing to do – to write him these beautiful letters.

One never hears Victor and Sonia talking to each other, and their interaction has to be inferred. The whole relationship seemed distorted to B. A. Young: 'he is a terribly selfish man ... Her strange way of writing to her husband through the post is no doubt due to his steady neglect of her'. Steady neglect is perhaps rather strong – Ted Whitehead was more precise in *The Spectator* in calling it 'a very old-fashioned, romantic patriarchal vision of what a man and woman can give to each other'. This, however, does not quite encompass the 'large self-assured presence' (*III* 199) of Sonia: Irving Wardle even saw Victor's decline as giving Sonia satisfaction, 'so that at last he is feeble enough for her to control'.

The disparity between the outward appearance of Sonia and her inner sense of herself rests on the impact of the letters; these are given by Victor to his friend Maurice to read but the audience hears them in voice-over read out by Sonia, so that we are admitted to her intimate thoughts while looking at her imperturbable, unsympathetic exterior – something the short story form could not put across as forcibly and simultaneously. Maurice, says the stage direction, '*looks at Sonia, with even greater bewilderment, seeing a different woman. So do we*' (*III* 205).

Maurice, a Professor of Art History, is the confidant of Victor's anxieties as well as being given the letters – a mechanism that seemed to creak a bit in both play and story. David Nathan put his finger on the logical weakness:

What is odd and disquieting is that neither of these two supposedly sensitive men feels any sense of betrayal at sharing these intensely private letters; the professor even goes so far as to read one that has been left unfinished on her table.

This objection seems valid – the play is after all naturalistic, and the handing over of the love letters, indeed the cavalier reference to them as 'mad', don't fit with Victor's supposedly perceptive character, and no doubt give rise to an impression of selfishness. Does the special licence given to Victor, and his self-absorption in the face of death, indicate sentimentality at the heart of the play? Frank Marcus thought that 'Wesker's assault on our tear ducts is too insistent' and Nicholas de Jongh also recoiled from the direct emotionalism: 'With the best will in the world, which I do not have, it is difficult to take seriously Arnold Wesker in a mood of reverent soppiness'. Benedict Nightingale was in a minority in considering that the emotion came off, largely because of the persuasive performance of Elizabeth Spriggs as Sonia:

> Michael Gough who plays her beloved, may seem to us to smell a little too strongly of sanctimony. To her he doesn't, and it is her view that finally and rather surprisingly prevails, partly because of Elizabeth Spriggs' po-faced mulish and utterly unposturing playing of the part, and partly because the love letters Wesker has concocted for her have a strange and haunting authenticity . . . Only Wesker, of our dramatists, would presume to prise the heart from its standard slot and hang it so openly on the sleeve. And only Wesker could get away with it.

But more critics thought that he got away with it in the television version in 1976, where Sonia was also played by Elizabeth Spriggs. Terms like 'compelling', 'absorbing' and 'skilful, tactful and passionate' were forthcoming, though Nancy Banks-Smith felt it was a radio play *manqué*:

> She comforts him with huge pillows like breasts, she stays him with strawberry jam and cream, and, as he grows weaker, her song grows stronger. As he dies of leukaemia she is singing like a bird: 'Your blood in my blood, rivers of it. Do you know it? Do you?' It gains everything from being heard and little, I think, from being seen.

Catherine Itzin found the television play moving, because intimate: 'With the camera we went inside her head, where the letters were her thoughts, as if whispered in his ear'. And she analysed what had changed in the tranference to the stage: 'Without the cameras to give direction, focus and emphasis, the professor's long, very visible silences while he listened to Victor's equally long, breast-beating soul searching speeches were conspicuous and distracting', and gave a static effect. There is the related question of pace, which had to be kept slow in Wesker's early plays, but if it is too slow the action loses all lightness of touch. Here the subject, as everyone commented, was mainly emotional, and needed the playing against the text that Wesker often advocates, the 'throwing away' that redeems self-analysis from self-indulgence. The character of Victor was based on that of Vic Feather, a former General Secretary of the Trades Union Congress who Wesker had known at one time: 'As a personality he appealed to me but one never knew his wife, and he never talked about her'. (Though Vic Feather did in fact die of leukaemia Wesker said 'I had no idea . . . that was a rather macabre coincidence – the original story was written long before I heard that news'.) As Benedict Nightingale said 'I suspect that that canny old gaffer might have been a bit embarrassed by so absolutely uncritical an obit' – so it seems that speed, restraint and astringency were present in the television production, but lacking in Wesker's own version on stage.

16

Caritas and *One More Ride on the Merry-Go-Round*

Though written over much the same period, these two plays could hardly be more different. When he had been writing *Golden City* and *The Four Seasons*, more or less at the same time, Wesker had separated them out as public and private areas of concern; here we have the comic and tragic sides of commitment, involvement, vocation – anything that turns into a straitjacket for the spirit.

Never having written a historical play until *The Merchant* – and given the traumas of that play, not a few of which had been connected with its historical background – it is surprising to find Wesker plunging straight back – further back, indeed – into history with the fourteenth-century setting of *Caritas*. It sprang from the germ of a story about an historical anchoress Christine Carpenter who had at her own wish been walled up in a cell by the village church, and then had changed her mind after three years and begged to be released. The church had refused and she had gone mad. Paul Levitt of the University of Colorado suggested that Wesker ought to write a play on the topic: writers are traditionally subject to a steady stream of helpful suggestions but in this case the germ turned into a 'vague idea' then into the 'idea for a play' in time to find support from three Scandinavian touring theatre companies. The three companies joined to offer Wesker a commission for the new play, and tentatively he began investigating the historical and religious background.

In September 1979 Wesker wrote in his notes:

I would like to write a simply constructed play which describes i) the act of immurement; ii) the anguish of those left behind – parents and boy-friend; iii) the moment of change of mind; iv) the effort to persuade the clergy to absolve her from her vow; v) their decision not to. Ending the first part with the church wall turning to reveal the terrified girl whom we see for the first time. Part Two consists of her stages towards madness. I don't want to enter into the psychology of the act or the girl. Something in the nature of the act – consisting as it does of retreat,

142

self-sacrifice and suffering – is there in us all. I simply want to create an archetypal story. In simple steps. With as little sophistry exchanged as possible. The decision, the act itself is so powerful that it carries its own resonance.

Later in his background reading he noted: 'Dangerously tempting to use history again. Must not forget intention of making the play a stark story of a young woman foolishly building walls around herself'. In his personal diary commented: 'It's like *The Merchant* all over again. All that reading'. So he was very aware of the pitfalls of excess historicism this time, and kept reminding himself of his criteria of simplicity and clarity – 'But the period can faintly simmer in the background'.

However, the powerful emotional predicament of the central character had to be paramount – as Wesker says, the impulses that drive Christine to self-sacrifice then cause her to revolt against it are familiar to everyone, and the situation of the historical anchoress provided a mythic image for such impulses. Here Wesker seems to have solved the problem he faced in *The Four Seasons* – how to make strongly emotional subject-matter as universal as possible, without either tying it to a specific and socially limited incident, or isolating the emotions in a kind of mysterious limbo. The anchoress's cell isolates Christine, and is in itself a rational pretext for presenting her isolation. The avoidance of too much psychologising also has a liberating effect on the theme: thus an individual emotional quirk is not presented as a general law of human nature. Wesker noted the 'need to avoid psychological explanations for her wish to be immured: the presence of a vividly identifiable reason for her wish becomes an alibi – "Oh, well, she suffered this as a child, understandable" – and thus it's difficult to identify with her wall because one can't share her background'.

Christine's initial confidence in her vocation is untroubled, and both innocent and touching in spite of the egotism with which she plays her role: 'I want my chains, I want my haircloth' (28). But it is not all egotism – she expresses a convincing love of the mystic's life, such as Wesker considered we can all respond to;

> There was a oneness time. I search that. When I were with my soul, an' my soul were with my body, an' my body were with me, an' we was all one with God an' His lovely nature an' there were O such peace an' rightness an' a knowin' of my place. That really were a oneness time that were. An' I search that, Lord Jesus. (26)

She has an ecstatic vision, following her appeal to the wood of the cross, which comes to her in the terms of her carpenter father's craft:

> It's a shape. The world's shape. I see its joins, what holds it together. I see the claspin's an' links. *There's* a dovetail. *There's* a mortice an' tenon. *There's* the hole an' there's the dowel. Oh! Oh! I see the harvest grow. I hear the flower blossom. I know the colour of the wind, the dark in light. There, there, before me, all joined an' locked an' fittin' an' rhymin'. There-is-no-mystery! I know the shape! Oh blessed merciful Jesus Christ, I prayed to the cross, an' the tree, an' the precious wood, an' you give me a showing. (35)

But this fades. Minutes later she can make no sense of what she had said. This is a turning point, and *'distressed and wild'* (38) she mocks her usual gossiping visitor Mathilde. We next hear that she is begging to be released, and the scene concludes with her voice crying 'Not fit! Not fit! Christine not fit!' and with the same force that she had demanded her hair shirt: 'Break down its walls, break them, break them. In the name of God BREAK THEM DOWN!' (44). The first act ends with the bishop's refusal to release her, and Christine's realization that her youthful enthusiasm has imprisoned her for life.

The second act is 'one continuous scene – in parts' (47). Immediately after writing it Wesker noted:

> Act Two is the strangest piece of writing I've ever committed to paper. It's a collection of moments divided by chants. There's a kind of sequence – moving from self-pity, to prayer, to pulling herself together, to light-headedness, to sexual ecstasy, to madness. I know what I want it to achieve – an experience. The experience of being a prisoner, of being locked up. A collection of moments, that's the best description. Are they the right moments, though? And does such a collection work, anyway?

It has to be the performance that turns the collection into a sequence. The 'parts' roughly define the 'moments', and they *'need to be divided by "puffs" of light fading in and out with sufficient darkness in between to allow Christine to move into a new framed position'* (8). The odd-numbered scenes among the first six simply show Christine repeating 'I ent narthin', I heve narthin', I desire narthin' save the love of Jesus only' over and over. In the National Theatre production, Patti Love muttered these lines, sitting hunched with her knees pulled up and clasped in her arms, rocking fast and rhythmically so that her bare feet slapped the floor in time to her chanting. The effect is not only of the passing of time but also of the aching monotony of imprisonment, and the audience cannot avoid the message that madness must be the end of this self-mortification.

Between these rituals come her outbursts. First she begs in calm, reasonable tones: 'Stands to reason, father. Honest. Believe me. The solitary hears the truth an' thaas more'n she can bear. No one's made to hear *all* the truth, father. Help me please' (48). Then she cunningly transforms an elementary religious doubt – 'What sense do it make to give trouble before gettin' to heaven when you can get people into heaven wi' no trouble?' (49) – into a heretical vision which ought to disqualify her from her vocation: 'There ent one God, there's two! (49). When this ploy fails, she makes a few attempts to cope with her situation: '*She* must *establish a routine*', but the way she tries and rejects a string of possible activities shows their inefficacity almost before she starts:

> *Pause. What next? She rises quickly and sits on her stool. Pause. What next? Rises. With the end of her dress she dusts the table, then stool, then the bed then the stool again. Pause. What next? She places the stool in a different position. Then another position. Then in another position. Pause. What next? . . . (53)*

She repeats obsessively 'The remedy for lust is the mortification of the flesh' and sinks into a trance-like meditation on the Passion. Her physical identification with the image – 'Put nails through me! Through my hands, my feet. Me! Me! Oh the ache, the ache, the helpless ache. I can't bear it! Can't bear it! Cannot. Oh, oh . . .' (57) – turns into a confused, semi-erotic physical reaction: '*she is squeezing one bare breast, part a caress, part a maternal longing*'. This in turn becomes an intense longing for the natural world she has walled out:

> I'm naked. My body open to the sky, my skin in the grass, sun on my breasts. I feel cool winds bring me the smell of the hawthorn and the wild mint. An' I see birds sweepin' and singin'. An' those clouds, those glorious, rollin' shapes, that sweet scene, that soft air – thaas not the devil's forms, I say. Forgive me, father, but I say thaas never the devil's forms. (58)

Throughout the play, at the end of certain scenes, '*like punctua-*

tions of comment, will be heard – loud or soft, vicious or sympathetic – the chanting of children. Like a street game' (20). They chant her name and: 'Had a vision, had a word, had a revelation yet?'. In the second act, the text also requires them to stick their hands through the little window of the cell, waving mockingly. At the very end of the play, the hands and chanting taunt Christine: '*Slowly she moves towards them. Watches. Then – she grabs one and plunges her teeth into it. There is a terrible scream*' (58). The last we see of her is as she stands, touching the wall, repeating 'This is a wall, an' this is a wall, an' this . . .'.

The shape of the play depends totally on the control of the emotion projected by Christine. Wesker at one point had doubts about his original concept of keeping the main external events to the first act 'and then just a second act of her descending into madness. I feel it may be out of balance'. In the National Theatre production the descent into madness did not in fact seem gradual and definitive enough. Act One ends with a *coup de théâtre* as the solidly walled, circular cell, into which Christine has disappeared in scene one, revolve to show us the interior, and Christine in it. The text says '*The sight of her is shocking. She is dirty, unkempt and terrified*' (46), and Wesker had also wondered about this: 'The verdict is "no", then we see her "dirty, unkempt and terrified". Won't her madness simply be an anti-climax? Isn't the sight of her enough?' The audience's impression would be that she was mad already: and as Wesker had said of Zero Mostel, it's necessary to start at the bottom if you're going to leave yourself somewhere to go. Therefore in the National Theatre production, Christine looked terrified, but not excessively bedraggled. However emotion is strongly present even in the earlier parts of Act Two – Christine's rapid movements are written into the stage directions, and her heretical 'vision', though it has its element of calculation, becomes a frenzied experience through her desperate desire to use it as a loophole to freedom. Patti Love's performance, quite intense even in Act One, reached its heights early in Act Two, and the second half became an anatomy of madness rather than a progress towards it. The original stage direction for the closing lines read:

She turns to the wall, places her hands on it, then moves along it, crossing one hand over the other, feeling the wall, even the imaginary walls, her hands crossing over, in space, as in mime, so that we 'see' the walls.

(The 'imaginary walls' are the fourth wall between Christine and us.) This was changed in production, 'so as not to have a false ending'. The director John Madden wanted to end the play just before this with a scream, and felt that any more moving about would imply that the play was going on. Wesker considered that the final compromise – a dying away, with Christine mumbling but immobile – gave the best of both worlds; but in practice it didn't convey any more of a nadir of madness than earlier mutterings or screams, whereas Christine endlessly feeling the wall might have given a more positive image of obsession.

Another alteration to the text may have worked against a sense of progressive dementia. For reasons of economy a recording, rather than real children, was used for the chanting voices, so there was no variation from tender to taunting. And of course there were then no children's hands, so no savage bite from Christine at the end – and just another scream from Christine did not have the climactic effect of such feral behaviour.

The intensity of the dialogue had to be carefully modulated, as Wesker realized early on: 'I left the manuscript with a high pitch ringing in my ears. Must watch that tone'; and he commented later 'how dangerous the language was'. In the event, the language was admired more than is usually the case with Wesker's plays – Milton Shulman thought the 'relentless moralizing' was redeemed by the 'vivid and virile dialogue', and Michael Coveney liked the 'monologue of frustration, hysteria and humanitarian common sense' of the second half where 'The play's prose takes flight, its rhythms and cadences leaping to life in Miss Love's virtuoso technical display'. Evidently the highly emotional subject matter had saved the play from accusations of dryness and excess argumentativeness, though Wesker himself had initially recoiled from the 'religion of pure emotion' endemic to his subject-matter. Noting a passage from *The Cloud of Unknowing* about the impossibility of knowing God by thinking about Him – 'He may well be loved, but not by thought. By love may he be gotten and holden, but by thought never' – Wesker rejected the possibility of contemplation without thought, along with other over-emotional elements:

Something to do with the transference of responsibility, or the elevation of dependence – which in other circumstances would be considered a

147

failing – into a high religious principle. And ecstasy – that absurd state of surrender! Three of the most pitiful human flaws – irresponsibility, dependence, surrender – all transformed into religious virtues. Ugh!

On the other hand, Evelyn Underhill's book *Practical Mysticism* began to win him to the opposite viewpoint, and renew the attraction towards mysticism he had once felt, and which he believed had wide appeal:

> A powerful book that leads me into the grip of the contemplative life. She seems to speak of a need I seem to feel. Certainly that mystic state, if it is achievable or if I could discipline myself to reach it, would answer the profound dissatisfactions which cause turmoil in me just now.

Having chosen what he thought would be 'a metaphor for the darkness of fanaticism' he began to see 'an area which promises light!'

Christine herself of course is seeking for light, and we have to see that it is less self-discipline than escapism. Looking back over Wesker's plays about waverers, betrayers, compromisers – characters whose enthusiasm fades or is worn down – one might wonder why this play is offering a totally opposite message: that enthusiasm is a mistake, and one should not be fully committed. Christine's predicament illustrates nicely the point that enthusiasm and commitment are secondary virtues, good or bad only according to their application, and that they can require perhaps too high a price. Christine's original dedication is wrong – it is too total and solves problems by shutting them out, unlike Dave's, Pip's, Andy's. Several critics invoked the shade of Beatie Bryant – perhaps because Christine is another such virtuoso part for an actress – Nicholas de Jongh called her 'a direct ancestor of Beatie Bryant' as 'each of them aspires to education and illumination, each conflicts with the dominating modes of the time'. John Elsom also saw her as trying 'to escape from the impoverished lives which her family led into one of greater enlightenment'. Christine's internal pilgrimage, however, is in the opposite direction from Beatie's – she starts by flinging herself into spiritual fanaticism, while the stolid Beatie spends most of her play resisting anything outside her very limited ambitions, then at the end, where Beatie breaks out of her shell and begins to relate to the wide world, Christine sinks into the deeper imprisonment of madness within her prison. The one point of comparable 'illumination' could be found in Beatie's breakthrough into understanding and Christine's belated recognition of the value of the world she has lost, but the significance of their discoveries is not the same. Wesker could not understand the comparison: 'they are quite different, their whole development is quite different'. Surely Benedict Nightingale was right in seeing Beatie as the absolute reverse of 'her ancestor' Christine, and the two women as respectively triumphant and defeated, though the moral he drew from the play – 'Extravagant hope ends in excessive despair' – should not be taken as nihilistic. This is indeed Christine's lesson, but it is not Wesker's own disillusion speaking, as his programme note states:

> Injustice cannot be tolerated but that does not mean the ideal is ever attainable.
> It is right not to tolerate injustice, but it is foolish to expect people ever to be perfect.

As the note explained, the play's background – dealing with the Peasants' Revolt – was intended to counterpoint Christine's experience. While the peasants make their doomed fight against social bonds, Christine willingly plunges into another kind of bondage. Everywhere man is in chains, and the perverseness of Christine's self-mutilation is nothing like Beatie's opening her mind to greater contact with humanity. Beatie's hope was not extravagant (because not formulated as dogma), and as for the peasants' uprising, this may have been extravagant, but, as the programme says, some things must be fought against; our feeling is one of regret for their failure, not regret that the attempt was made.

The actual presentation of the historical background did not satisfy many critics – the peasants 'ploddingly explaining how they have to plough and shear sheep unpaid for by the Church savours of a school play written for history juniors' objected John Barber. Avoiding the fullness of *The Merchant* had given an impression of baldness. Ned Chaillet thought the 'parallel' had not been dramatized fully: 'Wesker lets it happen so casually that the actors hardly bother to play any parts, clearly realizing that only one role was written for a performance'. In other words, the other peasants are a distraction from Christine's story. But it is important here that, unlike the protagonists of *The Four Seasons*, we see Christine's turning away from the outside world as part of the play, not

149

just a convention; she is preoccupied with her own problems while more serious struggles are going on. In this context her mysticism can more clearly be seen as escapism. There is a telling similarity with Roland in *The Friends*: he too tries to escape into detached contemplation or arbitrary self-injury from the pains of living. Wesker's repeated credo is that one has to make order out of the chaos of experience: ironically the Bishop uses the same phrase as an excuse for keeping Christine walled tidily away. Not all methods of making order are valid – in the Bishop's, and Christine's and Roland's cases, 'order' is merely an artificial simplification, which leaves out too much. It is not Wesker who is advocating easy extremes: on the contrary, as in all his plays, he is warning against them.

After this intense and harrowing historical play, *One More Ride on the Merry-Go-Round* is modern, sexy and funny. One thread of the plot may have some slight similarity to *Caritas*, in that immurement was intended as a metaphor for over hasty and crippling commitment to jobs, life-styles, marriages, responsibilities, politics – any limiting situation. In *Merry-Go-Round* Jason and Nita have just broken out of an imprisoning marriage, much of the angst of which has been a phantasm, in that both have secretly been longing for excitement and passion and blamed the other for being dull. Jason has also just, at the age of fifty, not escaped but been ejected from his imprisoning job as a philosophy lecturer, and though he is not exactly upset about this, he has a feeling that he ought to be. At least he would like some solid reason for returning within the walls of a safe job – or, alternatively, for *not* doing so.

If we look back at earlier Wesker characters – at Ronnie in *Chicken Soup* being urged to care or die, at Andrew Cobham's brave crusade for golden cities, and at all the lost, disillusioned strugglers, such as Dave and Ada, Pip, Boomy, whose failures to follow their early vocations are seen as tragic – this change to such insouciance, such readiness to pull up ones roots and become a rolling stone, borders on the incredible. Asked whether his last two plays stood as a rejection of vocation, Wesker was surprised: 'It's simply that at some time everyone has the wish to change their skin, be someone else doing something different'.

The two acts both begin in darkness: with Act One Jason is

Above: The Old Ones, with Max Wall (centre),
Royal Court, 1972. *Below: The Wedding Feast*, Leeds, 1977.

Above: The Merchant, New York, 1977.
Below: Patti Love in *Caritas*, National Theatre, 1981.

making love to Monica – even in the darkness we learn that she is much younger than him and he is a hypochondriac ('That's how I'll die. One day you'll come and I'll go').

The second part of the first act consists of Jason's fiftieth birthday party at which three of his not very friendly colleagues give answers to his question 'Why work?' One, Cecilia, replies: 'to eat', and adds that doing work that needs doing is its own justification; another, Anthony, says that as we need to have some work done, it is morally right for everyone to do their share; and the third, Montgomery, comes down on the side of work as an innate compulsion: 'it's an immutable law of human nature'. Jason is not moved by these general guidelines; he explains that, in his experience, following moral imperatives has always made him miserable. But his guests are no longer listening, because they have been eating birthday cake sent by his ex-wife Nita, into which she has baked what must have been quite a lot of marijuana. The party does not turn out as catastrophic as the *Wedding Feast* celebration, but it is far from the hero's expectations, and the curtain comes down on Jason cursing Nita amid confusion.

Nita meanwhile – also first introduced in bed with a much younger lover – is very happy with her life. She is absorbed in an unconventional campaign to 'Give a week's wages to the Third World', her love affair with Mat is going well, and moreover she has had cancer of the breast and survived it, a brush with death that has confirmed her appreciation of life. The theme of what Jason has called 'the demise of the work ethic' is continued in this Act through her daughter who at the fifth draft of the play is called Christine (though with nothing in common with her predecessor and namesake in *Caritas*). She is a photographer who doesn't like her job, and has just returned from a year in a kibbutz without any new inspiration about what to do with her life: 'nothing, nothing drives me sufficiently to make me get up and do'.

Christine's problem is solved by the arrival of Eckhard, her long lost illegitimate half-brother, the result of Jason's brief affair with a German lady while on a lecture tour twenty-five years earlier. Eckhard is an accomplished magician; Wesker's notes insist: 'The role of Eckhardt ought to be played by a brilliant conjurer who can act rather than an actor who learns tricks' and 'On no account must the performer be a secondrate magician'. Eckhard puts on a show for his new family, and 'this part of the play must be stunning'. The enraptured Christine is for the first time in her life carried away by a sense of vocation – to become a magician's assistant:

> Good photographers are ten a penny. I don't care about it. Don't you understand that? I just don't care, care, care! I want to be a magician!

That at least she cares about. Christine is of those, like Ada Kahn from the Trilogy and Jessica from *The Merchant*, who are content with their own few square inches of happiness and order, let the rest of the world be as chaotic as it will. Nita on the other hand reaches a balanced position between early Weskerian dedication and the dilettantism of Jason: she cares, because, as she says at first, 'I believe in a society where you help your neighbour because you love him'. She avoids the accusation flung at Sarah Kahn, about forcing strawberries and cream on everyone whether they like it or not, by later adding that one should 'leave him alone because you respect him'. And finally she makes this into a mature three-part credo – 'and know the right time to do which!'

Like many farces, this one ends with a lot of slamming doors as the characters pop in and out trying to have the last word: Christine is joining forces with Eckhard, and Monica agrees to accompany Jason on an indefinite exploration of the 'travel ethic', presumably throwing up her lectureship in history in the process. The formulation of Nita's 'help – but – let alone' principle is the one positive product of the play, though it is not strongly urged, not being attached to a major theme. This slight vagueness of direction had been noticed by Peter Hall, and Wesker wrote:

> Now think Peter Hall's observation is correct. By 'not centred' he means that the play has not quite made up its mind what it's about. This is because I simply set out to write something funny. In the process two themes shadowily emerged through which I plied the fun. Nothing wrong with these two themes providing one is the stronger, becomes the central drive. In Merry-Go-Round this doesn't seem to have happened. Is it about the way in which a couple blossom into what each wants the other to be only when they have separated? Or is it about the demise of the work ethic?

At the fifth draft the ending still seems not quite conclusive – a common feature of farces. While one can see how Jason's mock gloom could well have made Nita despair in his sexually unregenerate phase, it is not convincing that *he* could have seen *her* as 'dull' in *her* sexually unregenerate phase – even Christine's excuse for lack of ambition is that her mother's personality has swamped her: a bully, perhaps, but not dull.

Wesker had sent the fourth draft round to various managements and companies under an assumed name, and got some intriguing replies, ranging from enthusiastic interest to regret at his obvious lack of dramatic experience, but these, and the replies to another mailing under his own name produced no firm offer. So, at present a survey of Wesker's full-length plays ends with something of a Beechamesque 'lollipop' – but one which may never be tasted by the public.

17

Shorter Plays

This section looks briefly at Wesker's shorter plays, in chronological order: first, the festival play *The Nottingham Captain*, 1962; then the television play *Menace* screened in 1963; and finally passing over the television version of *Love Letters on Blue Paper*, discussed already in its stage version – a cluster of monologues and short plays completed in 1981.

THE NOTTINGHAM CAPTAIN

This short piece was 'compiled in a weekend in 1962 for the Centre Fortytwo Trade Union Festivals. The commission had been given to another writer, who let them down at the last minute'. Nottingham was in fact one of the festival towns. The subject is the prosecution of the machine-breakers in 1817, for an attempted uprising, largely triggered off by a 'Mr Oliver', a government *agent provocateur*. It is a promising blueprint for a Brechtian exposition of this incident – there are placards and songs – but as it stands it is not fully dramatized: its subtitle is 'a moral', and Wesker is careful to use the work 'compiled' rather than 'wrote'. The narrator tells the outline and background of the story and comments on it – 'Oh dear! The marvellous irony was – they could have done it. These twenty years in English history was the one period when they could really have had a revolution but – there were no leaders'. Mr Oliver and one or two others narrate their own part in the plot, and at one point Oliver makes a direct speech to the Nottingham Captain, Jeremiah Brandreth, who has no lines of his own apart from some verses of a song. The narrator reads out an account of the execution of Brandreth and his fellows from the *Gentleman's Magazine* – last words and all. Because of pressure of time, this remains in a transitional state between narrative and documentary drama, though it is interesting to compare it both with the German expressionist author Ernst Toller's *The Machine-Wreckers* (1922) – a 'drama of the English Luddites' also set in London and Nottingham and starting, as Wesker's piece does, with a version of the 1812 House of Lords debate between liberal Lord Byron and reactionary Lord Castlereagh – and with Wesker's later blend of narrator with fully dramatized action in *The Wedding Feast*. Wesker himself did not regard *The Nottingham Captain* as of great importance in his work.

MENACE

Wesker unwisely declared that *Menace* was to be 'an experiment on the result of which will depend whether or not he will continue to work in the television medium'. There was some bridling at this; for instance, the *Sunday Times* critic reacted indignantly to Wesker's approaching a mass medium as if it were savage territory to be colonized. But the main objection to the play itself was that it had little plot to speak of – though few commented on the equal plotlessness of *Love Letters* thirteen years later – and in spite of the title, there is very little menace to speak of either. The characters are mostly solitary bed-sit dwellers, and are 'menaced' by poverty, insecurity, and in one case, approaching blindness. The central couple, unemployed artist Garry and his rich girlfriend Harriet, show terror at the occasional deafening planes that pass overhead, and there is eventually overt but immediately quelled menace from three youths in the street – yet no *atmosphere* of menace as such develops. This is probably why, though the laconic, mundane dialogue *reads* like early Pinter, no critic found the production Pinteresque. Even the obvious power struggle between Garry and Harriet in the restaurant where she is treating him and three elderly neighbours to a meal does not have the Pinteresque aura of irrational and frightening hostility. As in *The Wedding Feast*, Wesker did not want overtones of the sadistic and the unnatural to creep in – his characters may have their irrational moments but they never become monstrous. The naturalistic, slice-of-life effect given by the first two-thirds of the play was preferred to the latter part, where Garry and Harriet take off on a whimsical odyssey through the city, paint a horse on a wall, and finally enter a club where they join in a warm, beautiful and evidently symbolic folk dance. Several critics suspected that there was far too much symbolism in the play, though John Russell Taylor in *The Listener* (admitting to his 'lack of sympathy with what Mr Wesker is trying to do in his drama and the way he sets about doing it') found in the images 'a poetic unpredictability, an unwillingness to force any neat formulation of their "meanings" upon us'. But otherwise critical opinion was unenthusiastic; and Wesker did not feel his experiment had indicated a promising career in television. There are hints of elements in later plays, particularly *The Old Ones*, in that short-sighted Sophie's lonely monologue is a little like Teressa's, and the three youths who follow her imitating her hobbling are precursers of the three who follow and attack Gerda. And Wesker adds that it contains 'the seeds of both Kate and Andy in *Golden City*, and Adam and Beatrice in *Four Seasons*', in Harriet's Kate-like arrogance, and in the couple's compulsive quarrels. But in cultivating these seeds, Wesker turned back to the theatre.

BREAKFAST

In 1976 Wesker turned his short story *Love Letters on Blue Paper* into a television play, and in 1980 he did the same for his short story *The Visit*, although it has never been produced. Also unproduced is an original television play, *Breakfast*. Set in present-day Munich, it deals with a few days in the life of Mark Bell, an English Jew, owner of a camping equipment factory, who is in the process of concluding a business deal. Prosperous, kindly, clean Germany – epitomized in his generous *pension* breakfast – is counterpointed with his reading from a Penguin edition of *If This is a Man* by Primo Levi, an account of the deportation of the Jews in Nazi Germany, extracts from which are read in voice over. Mark is not cultivating resentment or vindictiveness, as he explains to Frau Kettner, his business contact: 'I know it's unnatural, but I've never been able to get angry on behalf of the past, especially a past I didn't experience'. She herself is liable to preoccupation with vicarious remorse, as her lover, an Israeli also called Mark, teases her:' 'He thinks I've fallen in love with tears and guilt'. The two Marks take a more pragmatic view. After accompanying her on a visit to an old man, one of the very few survivors of ten thousand Jews killed in a certain town during the war – a gentle old man who does not rage – Mark Bell tells her: 'now you'll understand better why I don't rush into righteous anger and tragic tears. That old man has the moral authority to, and he didn't. How can I?' Yet during his final German breakfast, the cumulative effect of his book breaks down his emotional distance: '*Mark lowers his book. He is weeping. It is a shock to us, a shock to him*'. He flees to his bedroom,

156

trying to control himself, determined not to 'suffer by proxy'. But it is not easy. His face seems to be asking the question: where did it come from? Where? He even opens out his hands as though questioning a companion. It doesn't make sense. I was eating, unaffected, and then –

As always with Wesker, nothing is as simple as the rational man makes out.

ANNIE WOBBLER

Quite different are the 'Three modest monologues for the talents of my friend Nichola McAuliffe'. Where the television play, *Breakfast*, was highly visual – for long sequences, Mark is seen shopping, eating, comparing prices – the monologues necessarily depend on spoken words, and there is little use of props or business. The first monogue, *Annie Wobbler*, is spoken by a *'part-time tramp, part-time cleaning woman ... She must have once been maid in an upper-class household, her speech and manner carry the echoes of "refainment". The years of decline have made her eccentric'*. She is working for a poor Jewish family in the East End, cleaning for sixpence *'or some bread and tea. Whichever's around'*. Among her reminiscences about her sister and her first job she gives an account of her present family, various aspects being based on Wesker's own family (the prediction that he would be 'a great man or a murderer', his clever sister who 'talks posh', his childhood radio imitations under the eiderdown).

She then transforms herself into Anna, *'a strong young woman'*, examining herself in a mirror, dressed in a *' see-through slip beneath which is a black brassiere, panties, suspender-belt and stockings! Also black boots'*. This Anna defiantly proclaims her defences of knowledge, pausing occasionally to ask her reflection questions like 'But who are *you*? I've never seen you here before. Do you always go shopping like that?' She has to remind herself not to be ashamed of her intelligence: 'This tedious English habit of pretending ignorance', just as she keeps mocking at her appearance – but ends up *'ravishing'*, the stage direction tells us. But the attitude of Anna is triumphant – she is going out with a man whose faults she proceeds to list ('that way he'll be a pleasant surprise'), and who is going to be used as demonstration platform for her triumphant postgraduate self:

Because he's your first date since becoming a B.A. first class honours
and your cultural references shine like diamonds and you've broken the
stranglehold of those century-old genes of crass ineptitude and suppli-
cation and you've unknown muscles to flex and a lot of intimidating to
make up for and he's just the size and texture your teeth need sharpening
upon. Upon which your teeth need sharpening. Upon which your teeth
need! Upon which!

Poor fellow. Only perhaps she'd have broken the stranglehold
more entirely if she didn't feel the need to prove anything?

This Anna, in any case, is young, intelligent, witty, powerful
and beautiful – the opposite in all respects of Annie Wobbler. Of
course Wesker does not leave us with two unreconciled extremes
of womankind, but characteristically adds Annabella Wharton, a
creative writer whose initials are the same as his own, who gives
three quite contradictory interviews – assertive and dismissive,
scatty and vague, and finally resigned but insecure. Her fourth
novel has been a phenomenal success and when first asked what
drives her to write she snaps back, 'Fame Money and Power', and,
answering 'Have you any fears?', she winds up *'Defiantly smug'*
with 'Not now. None!' In her second persona, the question 'Could
you say what drives you to write?' gets the insouciant reply, 'Oh
my goodness me, no. Oh good Lord, no'; and as for her fears, she
pours out a stream of items – 'Everything frightens me. The
morning, the door-bell . . .' – which continues inexorably over the
interviewer's repeated 'Do you feel you have an endless flow of
material?' For the third interview, *'she's tired of play-acting. She's
tired'*. Her brief 'no' to being asked if she understands her compulsion to write is a sincere and painful 'digging for the inexplic-
able' and she has a few credible fears to offer. She concludes:

> My father used to have a 78 record of a song called 'Ah! Sweet Mystery
> of Life' and he'd put it on and it would get stuck at the 'myst'. (*Gently
> sings it*.) 'Ah sweet myst- sweet myst- sweet myst –' And then he'd push
> it and you'd get to 'life'. Well, I'm a bit like that. Stuck at the 'myst'.

Under the role-playing, without her shell, she is as bewildered as
any sensible human being ought to be. Necessarily these monologues provide an opportunity for an actress to show her versatil-
ity, but at the same time can, by their range, show the alternative
possibilities – of women's lives in general, and a writer's life in
particular. The form matches the content.

As with his latest full-length play to date, the most recent of Wesker's short pieces is a laugh-aloud comedy, written for Tokyo. Lynn and Malcolm are giving a dinner party, and when guests Stephen and Pam arrive, their host's first words are 'You take Pam into the lounge. Stephen, I want you in the loo'. The main action of the play in fact takes place inside the luxuriously appointed lavatory, thus making the play ideal for the cramped playing space of fringe and club theatres. It is some time before Malcolm explains what it is all about: 'What I am about to ask you to do may sound absurd but it's serious, though not without its humorous side'. He is so absorbed in his plan that he shows no recognition of the bizarre nature of his requests: '(*Intense. Concentrated.*) Stephen, what I want you to do is to show me exactly what you do when you go for a crap'. Much of the humour then is built up from the incongruity of Malcolm's seriousness and the conventionally delicate, if not taboo, nature of the subject. Added to this there is the embarrassment of the guinea-pig, and the surprising revelation of various idiosyncratic rituals. Eventually Malcolm reveals that his inspiration for making a lot of money relies on everyone having his own reaction – 'Urgh! I think – urgh! This hand! Sullied! Unclean! I can't bear to place it anywhere' – too sullied, he argues, even to use to adjust his dress, whatever it might be, flush the loo etcetera, all of which is usually done *before* washing the hands. Obviously one should have a dispenser of disinfectant-impregnated tissues – 'wet ones' – beside the toilet roll holder for instant accessibility. Stephen is not entirely convinced: 'But you must be the only person in the world who cares!' So the whole investigation is repeated with each of the other guests, two more of whom now arrive: 'Claudine! Just in time. Would you care to join Stephen and me in the loo?' (Her ritual involves 'hovering' in public lavatories: 'My mother always warned; on your own lav, your best friends' lav, your relatives' lav you may sit. In public lavs – hover!') Stephen remarks 'I must say, once people get into the spirit of it all, they do become inspired', and Claudine eventually agrees with Malcolm 'as a matter of fact, now you mention it, I've often wished the basin were nearer'. Pam is the next victim: she always carries newspaper to cover the entire floor of a public lavatory. Finally, Claude and Lynn explain their routine in duet – Lynn is by far the most inhibited and embarrassed about all aspects: it has to be 'at home. I never, never, never do it anywhere else. I'd rather die!' Claude turns on all the taps 'to drown out noise', Lynn opens all windows. As Claude later comments, 'I never knew. Entirely other lives are conducted in toilets'. And he has always been worried about the sullied hand problem, so much so that he carries a supply of tissues around with him – an ideal customer for Malcolm's 'own-loo' dispenser.

And as Malcolm is calculating that he will clear two million pounds within two years, Lynn brings her delayed but hugely successful high-rise soufflé into the loo.

Comment on this play would be superfluous. Except to note that in one important respect it echoes a recurrent phenomenon in Wesker's work: his tendency to use intimate autobiography as raw material for his plays. *Sullied Hands*, too, is based on an episode which took place in the Wesker household ...

18

Non-dramatic Work

Partly because he quite simply liked writing prose fiction, but partly also because he wanted to communicate without the intervention of actors and directors, Wesker has written short stories sporadically but persistently over the years. He would like in fact to write a novel, and his stories keep getting longer with the hope that he will creep up on a novel in this way. But some of his stories have moved across to the dramatic form: *Love Letters on Blue Paper* became a television play in 1976 and a stage play in 1978, the *The Visit* has also been adapted for television though not yet produced. *Pools*, one of his earliest stories introduced him to Lindsay Anderson and subsequently to the Royal Court Theatre when Wesker suggested it to Anderson as the basis for a film scenario. Having effected this introduction, *Pools*, like a catalyst, remained itself unchanged as the project proved too expensive. Its style is highly naturalistic and descriptive in its reconstruction of the life of an elderly London Jewish widow, Mrs. Hyams, weighed down by her uneventful, lonely routine, but whose mild change of scene – a holiday in a middle-class bed-and-breakfast household in a seaside village – is prematurely terminated by the pull of her regular habits (specifically her obsession with checking her football pools coupon). It may have been the descriptive detail that suggested realization on film; in the original story Mrs. Hyams's deep and only half-understood changes of feeling – humour, tears 'tired, aged ecstasy' – are spelled out verbally whereas they could more suitably be recorded without comment by camera close-up. And though Wesker like all dramatists has to find pretexts for verbalizing or visibly demonstrating, feelings, states of soul and so on, – in prose fiction he can describe them straightforwardly from what ever viewpoint he chooses. Nonetheless he still favours the more complex stage picture, with several elements co-existing simultaneously, which the one-word-at-a-time process of reading fiction cannot capture.

Love Letters, already discussed in its stage version, shows clearly what is gained and what is lost in adaptation from one medium to another. In the story Maurice, the younger friend of a dying trade union leader, Victor, is the first-person narrator, but becomes a rather silent and rudimentary confidant in the play, because he no longer has an interior monologue. Thus, what is lost is precise information which cannot be mimed, such as Maurice's memories of the past. Immediate emotional reactions, on the other hand, can be absorbed economically and efficiently by an audience, as with Victor's 'spectrum of emotions', which otherwise have to be spelt out rather laboriously in the short story:

> anxiety at my arrival – could he carry through the pretence; the pretence itself, of mock surprise and unspontaneous pleasure; the guilt for deceiving the woman to whom he was married; joy for the sunlight; the distress of coughing. [LL p. 46]

However the actual process of adapting both this story and *The Visit* Wesker found surprisingly easy. Of the latter he said in his diary:

> I typed almost all of it straight from the book, sensing as I went along what should be used and what rejected for the screen. Seems to have fallen into place as naturally and swiftly as I remember *Love Letters* did. And I did that the same way, typing it straight on to page. Began by hand – as with *The Visit* – then realized, why bother? Type it out at once. Most of it is the organization of dialogue already written.

The Visit is that of an English couple to the rural home of a younger Danish couple. The older pair, Raphael and Maddeau, are happy, mature and fulfilled, while Karl-Olaf and Janika are 'going through a difficult time', so that the relaxed atmosphere is punctuated by little squabbles; and the holiday mood also keeps getting undermined by reminders of the threatening world outside (e.g. a circular, advertising anti-terrorist devices, the site of a possible nuclear shelter). This is one of the longest stories, and is divided into mini-chapters, but as Wesker said:

> Trouble is, there's no plot, only the framework of a Whitsun holiday with moments. I collect moments hoping they're the right ones which, when put together, will have an effect. It's a bit like working in the dark.

The visit accumulates happy moments as well as quarrels – a bicycle ride, a meal out, sunbathing, cooking, and by the time Raphael and Maddeau leave, the friendship has come to a moment of affirmation while listening together to music: 'Four friends with fibrillous lives, crazy patterns of trial and error, had woven that magic design of trust upon which wonder-full experiences rest' (LL p. 204), a sustaining experience, as so often in Wesker's work, to set against the doubts; and the younger couple seem to have rounded the corner of their 'difficult time' as well. The simultaneity of the stage moment is not there – but the exact selection of elements can be brought to the reader's attention: 'Colours sharpened off one from another . . . the table jumped, alive with differing shapes of cups, jam-jars . . . Maddeau moved on air. It seemed as if she was iridescent'. As Margaret Drabble said, the reader sees what the author wants him to see.

Repeating his earlier point, Wesker defined himself as 'a writer of moments, not narrative. I assemble moments and hope that placed as they are they assume a significance'. If not narrative, most of his stories move from *A* to *B* – a problem is solved, a process completed. In *Said the Old Man to the Young Man* there is a contrast of values between Martin, an aged, heavy, deaf Jew, visiting his family in London, and his great-nephew Amos, university-educated, who does not believe in any but logical and material values – though significantly he repeatedly becomes involved with beautiful intelligent humanist girls. Then the offer of a job in America with great prospects coincides with his present girl-friend's discovery that she has cancer and must have a breast removed. Should Amos go or stay – stay to do what, comfort her with sentimental gestures? He tries to reason it out, but suddenly it occurs to him that he has been brought up irrevocably moral – his logic cannot alter his conscience. And only after this does it occur to him that he may be really in love with this girl-friend. But Amos's glow of pleasure and relief at his moral decision to stay with her is juxtaposed with his great-uncle's having to wait for him alone outside the synagogue in the cold and rain. This is Amos's fault, because he has arrogantly taken the word of the 'expert' caretaker for the time the service finishes, instead of believing his old-fashioned great-uncle. He still has some way to go before he miraculously transforms himself into a truly good man. There is a narrative progression here, and a nice balance between the deliberately annoying old man and the arrogant young one – similar, though less obviously stark, to the dialectic of the brothers in *The Old Ones*. Some of the material from this story was, indeed, to reappear in *The Old Ones*, for Martin's relatives and friends include a Sarah, Teressa and Millie, named and characterized as in the later play.

In *The Man Who Became Afraid* there is again a progression, though towards failure this time. Quite a lot of dramatic plot material is compressed into an introductory two pages, including an account of the hero Sheridan Brewster and his youthful globe-trotting, his gun-running exploits, his studies and business, plus a one-paragraph vignette of Mildred whom he marries. His 'becoming afraid' happens in fits and starts. At first his being 'afraid of everything' is a joke. Later he clutters the house with fire-fighting appliances and patent medicines; and anxiety about the future impels him to collect and hoard goods as an investment and pile up insurance policies. Mildred's temporary concern and affection, after twenty-five years of an unhappy marriage, fade as she realizes his appeals to her spring from egotistic panic. When much younger, Wesker had been influenced by D. H. Lawrence, and this story has a Lawrentian theme to it, as Sheridan finally disintegrates from his own lack of real identity, his wife turning away to save herself from his desperate, vampire-like clutching at her. *Six Sundays in January* is more deliberately episodic in structure as the title suggests, consisting of a series of six Sundays in the life of Marcia, a thirty-five year old, well-to-do Jewish Hampstead housewife. The six Sundays do chart her gradual realization that she is getting older and no longer loves her husband, but there is less a sense of progression than a crystallization of knowledge already there. This depressing realization is given focus by the unexpected suicide of a friend for much the same reasons. Marcia ends with the acceptance of 'the pity of it and the sadness and the waste and the unimaginable pity of it' (SS p. 140) without a positive 'moment' as in *The Visit* or *Said the Old Man* to sustain her. The story seems to have less coherence, literally in the sense of unifying force, than the others – it may be an example of Wesker's 'moments' which have not quite coalesced into a whole.

The Man Who Would Never Write Like Balzac is a slighter work though with ironic humour and some autobiographical elements. A young Jewish silversmith, Constantine Lander, wants to be a great writer and sells the occasional poem or play, but mostly collects rejection slips. He is left at the end of the story gazing at a sheet of white paper, frustrated – but definitely a potential writer. The vivid and funny pictures of Constantine's home life, particularly the dialogue of his gentle, intelligent, defeated father are based on Wesker's own home and father, and could easily be transferred in chunks into *Chicken Soup*.

Some of Wesker's non-fiction works are mentioned elsewhere in this study – notably *Fears of Fragmentation*, the collection of lectures and articles that traces the progress of Centre Fortytwo; and *Journey into Journalism*, his account of the two months he spent at the *Sunday Times* gathering material for his play *The Journalists*. Characteristically, these pieces, whatever topics or issues they may be urging, constantly revert to personal experience and to a personal tone of voice. Even his pamphlet *Words*, arguing that a core of essential words for essential concepts ('Vindictive. Lilliputian. Mockery. Superficial. Spurious. Greed. Relativity. Tolerance. Doubt. Reason. Faith. Freedom. Demogogue. ... A linguistic survival kit!')[1] should be taught to all children, begins and ends with an anecdote about his son, then thirteen, being bullied at school. The *London Diary for Stockholm* is a more public version of the diary he keeps and has always kept: he says 'one of the reasons I waste time writing this diary (if I haven't already said this) is that I imagine the random record will, in its final totality, make a sense that I can't make of moment to moment'. Little incidents are transferred from his life as recorded in his diary into art; thus the long story of an American acquaintance's tracing the last climb of her dead son becomes a brief image in *Caritas*, and conversation with 'the wife of a friend who was on a lecture tour in the States and decided not to return' supplied the story line for a film script, *Lady Othello*. In all senses, there is a continuousness about the life and work of Arnold Wesker, and it is intentional:

> I would like people to know me not only by my writing but by my life; to know not only my writing but the writing of my contemporaries; to know not only literature but music and painting also; not only to experience art but to know how it came about and the times in which it came about and what else happened in those times, and the currents of religion, philosophy and science which shaped him and the clues which there are for him to understand so that tomorrow's revolution will not be an ugly but a noble one. (SS p. 186)

Notes

1: A Personal Tone of Voice

1 Interview with Maureen Cleave in *Observer Magazine*, 4 October 1981.
2 Michael Kustow, *Event*, 1 October 1981.
3 Interview with Robert Muller in *Harper's Bazaar*, October 1960.
4 *Ibid.*
5 For an account of the rise and decline of the Centre Fortytwo project, see Frank Coppieters, 'Arnold Wesker's Centre Fortytwo: a Cultural Revolution Betrayed', *TQ* V, 18, 1975, pp. 37–51.

2: Author, Director, Critics

1 Arnold Wesker, 'Debts to the Court', in Richard Findlater (ed.), *At the Royal Court – 25 Years of the English Stage Company*, Amber Lane Press, 1981, p. 81.
2 *The Times Saturday Review*, 5 August 1972.
3 *Ibid.*
4 *Ibid.*
5 *Ibid.*
6 Arnold Wesker, 'Butterflies with Everything', *Guardian*, 9 August 1972.
7 *Ibid.*

11: Watershed

1 Arnold Wesker, 'The Strange Case of the Actors' Revolt', *Sunday Times (Weekly Review)*, 30 August 1981.
2 *Guardian*, 13 May 1974.
3 Interview with Nigel Lewis, *Guardian*, 18 June 1974.
4 *Sunday Times (Weekly Review)*, 30 August 1981.
5 *Ibid.*
6 *Ibid.*
7 *Guardian*, 18 June 1974.

14: The Merchant

1 Arnold Wesker, 'Why I Fleshed Out Shylock', *Guardian*, 29 August 1981.

18: Non-dramatic Work

1 Arnold Wesker, *Words*, Writers and Readers Co-operative, 1976, p. 14.

Plays Produced

The Four Seasons (written 1964)
First performed at the Belgrade Theatre, Coventry, August 1965, directed by Henrik Hirsch. This production re-directed by Arnold Wesker, transferred to the Saville Theatre, London, 21 September 1965.

Their Very Own and Golden City (written 1963–5)
First performed at the National Theatre of Belgium, Brussels, directed by Jean Claude Huyens. First London production at the Royal Court Theatre, 19 May 1966, directed by William Gaskill.

The Friends (written 1967)
First performed at the Stadsteatern, Stockholm, 23 January 1970, directed by Arnold Wesker. First London production at the Roundhouse, 19 May 1970, directed by Arnold Wesker.

The New Play (written 1969)
No performance to date (1982).

The Old Ones (written 1970)
First performed at the Royal Court Theatre, London, 8 August 1972, directed by John Dexter.

The Journalists (written 1971)
First performed at the Criterion Theatre Coventry, in an amateur production, directed by Geoff Bennett. First professional production at the Landesbühne, Wilhelmshaven, Germany, 10 October 1981, directed by Klaus Hoser.

The Wedding Feast (written 1972)
First performed at the Stadsteatern, Stockholm, April 1974, directed by Gun Arvidsson. First British production at the Leeds Playhouse, 20 January 1977, directed by John Harrison and Michael Attenborough.

The Merchant (written 1974–6)
First performed at the Royal Dramaten Theatre, Stockholm, 8 October 1976 directed by Stefan Roos. New York premiere, 16 November 1977, directed by John Dexter. British premiere, 12 October 1978, at Birmingham Repertory Theatre, directed by Peter Farago.

Love Letters on Blue Paper (adapted from short story written 1974, already adapted as a television play 1976)
First performed in Syracuse, New York directed by Arthur Storch; British premiere, 15 February 1978 at the National Theatre, directed by Arnold Wesker.

Caritas (written 1979–80)
First performed at the National Theatre London, 7 October 1981, directed by John Madden.

One More Ride on the Merry-Go-Round (written 1978)
No performance to date (1982).

Sullied Hands (written 1981)
No performance to date (1982).

Annie Wobbler: Monologues for an actress (written 1981)
No performance to date (1982).

TELEVISION PLAYS
Menace.
Transmitted by BBC Television, December 1963, directed by Herbert Wise.

Love Letters on Blue Paper.
Transmitted by BBC Television, 2 March 1976.

The Visit.
No production to date (1982).

Breakfast.
No production to date (1982).

FILM SCRIPTS
The Kitchen.
Film made by unit of film technicians union (ACTT), directed by Jimmy Hill, released 1961.

Master (based on 'An Unpleasant Predicament', a short story by Dostoevsky, later developed into stage play, *The Wedding Feast*).
No production to date (1982).

Madame Solario.
No production to date (1982).

Brighton Belle.
No production to date (1982).

I'm Talking About Jerusalem (film version of the Wesker Trilogy).
No production to date (1982).

Select Bibliography

[*For a comprehensive bibliography up to 1977, see Glenda Leeming*, Theatre Checklist No. 14: Arnold Wesker, *London: TQ Publications, 1977*]

STAGE PLAYS

Collections

Arnold Wesker Volume 1, London: Penguin, 1981. Revised reprint of *The Wesker Trilogy*, London: Cape, 1960; New York: Random House, 1961; London: Penguin, 1964. Contains the Wesker Trilogy, i.e. *Chicken Soup With Barley, Roots, I'm Talking About Jerusalem*. Referred to as *I*.

Arnold Wesker Volume 2, London: Penguin, 1981. Revised reprint of *Three Plays*, London: Penguin, 1976. Contains *The Kitchen, The Four Seasons, Their Very Own and Golden City*. Referred to as *II*.

Arnold Wesker Volume 3, London, Penguin, 1981. Contains *The Friends, The Old Ones, Love Letters on Blue Paper*. Referred to as *III*.

Arnold Wesker Volume 4, London: Penguin, 1981. Contains *The Journalists, The Wedding Feast, The Merchant*. Referred to as *IV*.

Individual plays

The Kitchen, in *New English Dramatists 2*, London: Penguin, 1960. Revised version, London: Cape, 1961; New York: Random House, 1961; also in *Three Plays* (Shaffer, Wesker, Kops), London: Penguin, 1968; also in Arnold Wesker, *Three Plays* (with *The Four Seasons* and *Their Very Own and Golden City*), London: Penguin, 1976. Revised again for *I*.

Chicken Soup With Barley, in *New English Dramatists 1*, London, Penguin, 1959; also in *I*.

Roots, London: Penguin, 1959; and in *The New British Drama*, ed. Henry Popkin, New York: Grove, 1964; also in *I*.

I'm Talking About Jerusalem, London: Penguin, 1960; also in *I*.

Chips With Everything, London: Cape, 1962; New York: Random House, 1962; also in *New English Dramatists 7*, London: Penguin, 1963; and in *The Best Plays of 1963–64*, ed. Henry Hewes, New York: Dodd Mead, 1964; also in *III*.

The Nottingham Captain. A Moral for Narrator, Voices and Orchestra, in *Six Sundays in January*, London: Cape, 1974.

The Four Seasons, London: Cape, 1966; also in *New English Dramatists 9*, London: Penguin, 1966; also in *II*.

Their Very Own and Golden City, London: Cape, 1966; also in *New English Dramatists 10*, London: Penguin, 1967; also in *II*.

The Friends, London: Cape, 1970; also in *III*.

The Old Ones, London: Cape, 1973. Revised version: London: Blackie (Student Drama Series), 1974; also in *III*.

The Journalists. First published in Polish in *Dialog* (1974). In English: London: Writers and Readers Co-operative, 1975; also in *The Journalists – A Triptych*, London: Cape, 1979; also in *IV*.

The Merchant, in *IV*. Revised version: London: Methuen (Methuen Student Editions), 1983.

Love Letters on Blue Paper (stage version), London: TQ Publications (New Plays Series), 1977; also in *III*.

Caritas, London: Cape, 1981.

TELEVISION PLAYS

Menace. First draft published in *Jewish Quarterly*, Spring 1963. Final version in *Six Sundays in January*, London: Cape, 1971.

FICTION

Collections

Six Sundays in January, London: Cape, 1971. Referred to as *SS*.

Love Letters on Blue Paper, London: Cape, 1974. Referred to as *LL*.

Said the Old Man to the Young Man, London: Cape, 1978. Referred to as *SOM*.

Love Letters on Blue Paper and Other Stories, London: Penguin, 1980. Referred to as *LLOS*.

Individual Stories

'Pools', *Jewish Quarterly*, IV, 2. Also in *SS*.

'Six Sundays in January', *Jewish Quarterly*, XVII, 2. Also in *SS* and *LLOS*.

'London Diary for Stockholm', in *SS*.

'The Man Who Became Afraid', in *LL* and *LLOS*.

'A Time of Dying', in *LL*.

'Love Letters on Blue Paper', in *LL* and *LLOS*.

Say Goodbye! You May Never See them Again (text to accompany a book of paintings by John Allen), London: Cape, 1974.

'The Man Who Would Never Write Like Balzac', *Jewish Quarterly*, XXIII, 1 and 2, and in *SOM*.

Fatlips: a story for Young People (illustrated by Oscar Zarete), London: Writers and Readers Cooperative; New York: Harper and Row, 1978.

'Said the Old Man to the Young Man', in *SOM*.

'The Visit', in *SOM* and *LLOS*.

ARTICLES AND ESSAYS

Collections

Fears of Fragmentation, London: Cape, 1970. Referred to as *FF*.

The Journalists – A Triptych. London: Cape, 1979. Referred to as *JAT*.

Selected individual articles

'Let Battle Commence', *Encore*, V, 4, 1958; also in Charles Marowitz, Tom Milne and Owen Hale (eds.), *The Encore Reader*, London: Methuen, 1965; re-issued as *New Theatre Voices of the Fifties and Sixties*, London: Eyre Methuen, 1981.

'To React – to Respond', *Encore*, VI, 3, 1959.

'Vision, Vision Mr Woodcock' (on Resolution 42), *New Statesman*, July-August 1960.

'O Mother Is It Worth It?', published as a 'special' by the Oxford student magazine *Gemini*, 1960; also in *FF*.

'Two Snarling Heads', a lecture given in 1961, in *FF*.

'Resolution 42', *New Statesman*, April 1961.

'The Secret Reins', *Encounter*, March 1962; also in *FF*.

'The Allio Brief' (for Centre Fortytwo), *The London Magazine*, August 1965; also in *FF*.

'Fears of Fragmentation', a lecture given in 1968, in *FF*.

'Casual Condemnations', *Theatre Quarterly* II, 2, 1971.

'From a Writer's Notebook', *Theatre Quarterly*, II, 6, 1972.

'Butterflies with Everything', *Guardian*, 9 August, 1972.

'A Cretinue of Critics' (an open letter to Harold Hobson on his review of *The Old Ones*), *Drama*, Winter 1972.

'Unhappy Poisons' (reply to John Russell Taylor's review of *The Old Ones*), *Plays and Players*, November 1972.

'How to Cope with Criticism', *Plays and Players*, December 1972 (also a letter published in the same issue).

'The Playwright as Director', *Plays and Players*, February 1974.

'Words – as definitions of Experience' (Published with that title, along with 'Finding One's Own Voice', and 'afterword' by Richard Appignanesi), London: Writers and Readers Co-operative, 1976.

Journey into Journalism, London: Writers and Readers Co-operative, 1977; also in *JAT*.

'A Journal of *The Journalists*', *Theatre Quarterly*, VII, 26, 1977; also in *JAT*.

'Debts to the Court' in Richard Findlater (ed.), *At the Royal Court*, Ambergate: Amber Lane Press, 1981.

'Why I Fleshed Out Shylock', *Guardian*, 29 August 1981.

'The Strange Affair of the Actors' Revolt', *Sunday Times Weekly Review*, 30 August, 1981.

POEMS

'The Poor', *Plan*, March, 1952.

'Time Parts the Memory', *Jewish Quarterly*, Winter 1959–60.

'The Book in my Hand', *Overland* (Melbourne), 18, 1960.

'My Child', *Overland* (Melbourne), 1960. Also in *The Sixties*, Spring 1961.

'I Walk the Streets of Norwich', *Konkret* (Hamburg), 20, October 1961.

'Sitting Waiting for Auntie Anne' *Stepney Words*, 2, 1971.

'You Love Me Now', *Contrasts* (Shiplake College), 1972.

'Sebastian', in Spike Milligan and Jack Hobbs (ed.), Milligan's Ark, London: M & J Hobbs, 1977.

'It Was a Time of Feast and Weddings', *Piano*, Opus 1, Pushkin Press, Washington DC, July 1978.

'Not the Same', *Jewish Chronicle*, 28 December 1979.

'For a Friend, Lisa', *Write Thru the Year* (an anthology), edited by Nigel Gray, Northampton Press, 1980.

'The Confidence of Boughs', *Jewish Chronicle Literary Supplement*, 6 June 1980.

'The Clouds Are Low', *Jewish Chronicle Literary Supplement*, 28 December 1980

INTERVIEWS

In *The Times*, 21 September 1959. With Laurence Kitchin. Also in Laurence Kitchin, *Mid-Century Drama*, London: Faber, 1960.

In *Playbill*, 1964. With Walter Wager. Also in Walter Wager, *The Playwrights Speak*, New York: Delacourt Press; Harlow: Longman, 1968.

In *Tulane Drama Review*, XI, 2, 1966. With Simon Trussler. Also in Charles Marowitz and Simon Trussler (eds.), *Theatre at Work*, London: Methuen, 1967; New York; Hill and Wang, 1968.

In Ronald Hayman, *Arnold Wesker*, London: Heinemann, 1970. Two interviews with Ronald Hayman.

In *Transatlantic Review*, 48, Winter 1973–74. Ronald Hayman interviews Arnold Wesker and John Dexter jointly. Also in *Playback 2* ed. Ronald Hayman, London: Davis-Poynter, 1974. Shorter version: *The Times Saturday Review*, 5 August 1972.

In *Theatre Quarterly*, VII, 28, 1977. With Catherine Itzin, Glenda Leeming and Simon Trussler.

In *Tribune*, 13 October 1978. With Catherine Itzin.

SECONDARY LITERATURE

Books

Harold U. Ribalow, *Arnold Wesker*. Twayne's English Author Series, New York: Twayne Publishers, 1965.

Michael Marland, ed., *Arnold Wesker*. Times Authors Series No. 1, London: Times Education Services, 1970.

Ronald Hayman, *Arnold Wesker*. Contemporary Playwrights Series, London: Heinemann 1970. The American edition is updated with additional chapters: New York: Ungar, 1973.

Glenda Leeming and Simon Trussler, *The Plays of Arnold Wesker*. London: Gollancz, 1971.

Glenda Leeming, *Arnold Wesker*. Writers and their Works Series, London: Longman, for the British Council, 1972.

Selected Articles

John Dexter, 'Working with Arnold', *Plays and Players*, April 1962.

John Dexter, 'Chips and Devotion', *Plays and Players*, December 1962.

Laurence Kitchin, 'Theatre in the Raw', in *Mid-Century Drama*, London: Faber, 1962.

Laurence Kitchin, 'Drama with a Message: Arnold Wesker', in William A. Armstrong (ed.), London: Bell, 1963.

John Garforth, 'Arnold Wesker's Mission', in Charles Marowitz, Tom Milne and Owen Hale (eds.), *The Encore Reader, op. cit.*

John Russell Taylor, 'Productions out of Town', in *Anger and After*, London: Methuen, revised edition, 1969.

Malcolm Page, 'Whatever Happened to Arnold Wesker? His Recent Plays', *Modern Drama*, XI, 1968.

Garry O'Connor, 'Wesker: A Voice Crying in the Wilderness', *Sunday Times Colour Supplement*, 10 May 1970.

Garry O'Connor, 'Production Casebook No. 2: Arnold Wesker's *The Friends*', *Theatre Quarterly*, I, 2, 1971.

John Russell Brown, 'Arnold Wesker: Theatrical Demonstration', in *Theatre Language: a Study of Arden, Osborne, Pinter, and Wesker*, London: Allen Lane, The Penguin Press, 1972.

Michael Billington 'When Did You Last See Your Arnold Wesker?' *Guardian*, 13 May 1974.

Nigel Lewis, 'The Continuing Struggle ...', *Guardian*, 18 June 1974.

Frank Coppieters, 'Arnold Wesker's Centre Fortytwo: A Cultural Revolution Betrayed', *Theatre Quarterly*, V, 18, 1975.

Michael Billington, 'Wesker Bounces Back', *Guardian*, January 1977.

Catherine Itzin, 'Arnold Wesker', in *Stages in the Revolution*, London: Eyre Methuen, 1980.

Glenda Leeming, 'Articulacy and Awareness', in C. W. E. Bigsby (ed.), *Contemporary English Dramatists*, Stratford-upon-Avon Studies 19, London: Edward Arnold, 1981.

Index